THE MIGHTY MARS ROVERS

THE MIGHTY MARS ROVERS

The Incredible Adventures of Spirit and Opportunity

By Elizabeth Rusch

SCHOLASTIC INC.

ISBN 978-0-545-66320-5

12 11 10 9 8 7 6 5 4 3 2 1   13 14 15 16 17 18/0

Printed in the U.S.A.   40

First Scholastic printing, October 2013

Design by Ellen Nygaard
The text of this book is set in Proforma
Photo and illustrations credits on pages 78-79

Author's Note:

ON THE USE OF PRONOUNS FOR THE ROVERS

As an inanimate object, a Mars rover would generally be referred to as "it." The scientists and engineers who work on the rovers commonly refer to them as "she." For a more gender-balanced usage and to help readers distinguish between the two rovers, the author has decided to refer to Spirit as "she" and Opportunity as "he."

For Craig

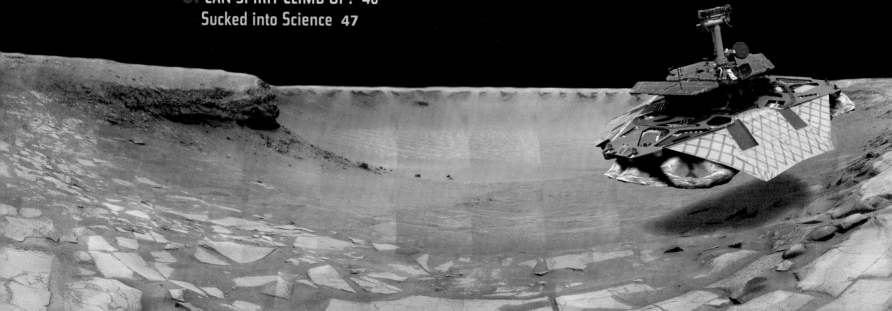

This view of Mars was captured by the Hubble Space Telescope.

Mars Exploration Rover Mission

Earth year: 2004

Explorers: Twin rovers Spirit and Opportunity

Leader: Steven Squyres, principal science investigator

Goal: To seek evidence that Mars once had water that could have supported life

Duration of the mission: Three months, maybe more . . .

The Search for Life on Mars

Are Martians real? As silly as it may seem, this question has driven Mars exploration for decades. People all over the world yearn to know: Is there life on Mars? If not, has there *ever* been life on Mars?

No one is seriously searching for green people with wobbly arms and bug eyes. If such creatures existed, we'd likely have found evidence of them by now. Instead, scientists are looking for much smaller, nearly invisible life forms—tiny creatures like bacteria and amoebae.

Why do so many people care about whether microscopic blobs have ever made a home on Mars, especially if they're not even alive anymore? Martians like these aren't going to invade our planet or steal our brains.

We care because we wonder: Did the miracle of life happen only once, here on Earth? Or is life something that can happen anytime the conditions are right? If some kind of living things, even very tiny creatures, once lived on Mars, then imagine what else may be living out there on the millions of billions of planets in our vast universe.

No life form known to us today can exist without water. So our search for life begins with the search for water . . .

1 Mission Impossible

On July 20, 1969, a thirteen-year-old boy named Steven Squyres watched in wonder as the Apollo mission put people on the moon. But the teenager didn't think the moon landing had much to do with him. "I loved watching it," he said. "But it was something people on television did. I didn't see it as something I could do."

Steve Squyres, age eight, gets his first telescope for Christmas.

At age nine, Steve tries to build his first robot.

Young Steve stands on top of a mountain near a pile of rocks.

Apollo 11 astronaut Buzz Aldrin walks on the surface of the moon.

Mariner 9, the first spacecraft to orbit another planet, was launched on May 30, 1971, and arrived to Mars's orbit on November 14, 1971. Scientists wondered whether the gash in this photo taken by *Mariner 9* was a canyon once carved by water.

At the time of the first moonwalk, scientists thought there was little chance of finding signs of life on Mars. In photos sent by the early Mariner spacecraft as they flew by Mars, the red planet looks lifeless, nothing but dust and old craters. But in 1971, when Steve Squyres was in high school, images from *Mariner 9,* the first spacecraft to circle Mars, tantalized scientists with what looked like huge canyons and empty channels—carved out earlier, perhaps by water, a key ingredient for life. Mars became a subject of great interest.

While Steve was finishing up high school, Russia and other countries tried to get a closer look at the dry rivers and lakebeds on Mars. They rocketed machines called landers to the planet's surface. Some crashed on impact. Some landed safely but then broke. Others missed the planet altogether. Five tries, five failures.

Steve headed off to Cornell University. He thought he might be a geologist. He enjoyed climbing mountains and had a knack for science. Geology, he thought, would be a great way to combine those interests. "But after studying geology for a while, I realized that people had figured out a lot of stuff on Earth pretty thoroughly," he said.

Then in 1976, the United States successfully landed *Viking 1* and *Viking 2* on Mars. Steve was a tall, lanky, hiking-boot-wearing college junior when he signed up for a class on the Viking mission. The class was taught by a working member of the Viking science team. "Suddenly, I was talking to people who actually *did* space exploration," Steve said. "I thought, *Wait a minute, maybe this is something* I *can do.*"

Steve loved all the fieldwork he did inside and outside the geology classes he took at Cornell University.

While a college student, Steve climbed Iztaccihuatl (Ixta) in Mexico.

Steve had to pick a topic for his term paper. He asked for a key to the Mars Room, a deserted, messy storage space with shelves of three-ring binders and long rolls of photographic paper full of images from the Viking mission. He thought he might spend fifteen minutes flipping through photos for inspiration. "Instead, I was in that room for four hours, racing through the pictures, stunned," he said. "I understood nothing that I saw, of course, but that was the beauty of it. *Nobody* understood most of this stuff. In fact, only a handful of people in the world had ever seen it yet."

Steve stared at one photo in particular: it showed a sunken area in Mars's red, dusty landscape, with fingerlike valleys flowing into it. To Steve it was obvious that the area had once been a lake. "But even more obvious was the fact that the Viking landers were not the right way to do planetary geology," he said. In Steve's geology courses, he had wandered through rock formations, picking up samples, touching, crushing, and testing rocks and soil. He carried a hammer for breaking up rocks. If he needed to dig, he dug.

This Viking orbital view of Mars shows the Valles Marineris canyon system, which looks like it was carved by water. The system is more than 1,846 miles long (3,000 km) and averages 5 miles (8 km) deep.

Viking 1 orbited Mars for a month before the lander separated and touched down on the red planet.

"Viking landers were not the right way to do planetary geology."

Viking 2 landed on Mars on September 3, 1976, some 4,600 miles from its twin, *Viking 1,* which touched down on July 20. Neither could move from their landing sites.

Steve devoted his undergraduate studies to planetary science. By the time he was in graduate school at Cornell, he was an associate of the Voyager imaging team, studying data and photos from Jupiter and Saturn.

But when Steve became a professor of astronomy at Cornell, exploring Mars was still what he wanted to do. "Just once," he said, "I wanted to create something from the start, to take it from the sketch of an idea to scientific discovery, with everything along the way."

With his knowledge of space imaging, Steve pulled together a team of scientists and engineers to build a special camera to send to Mars. "You start off with nothing but a bunch of smart colleagues and a vague idea of what you hope to accomplish, and then a concept starts to come together before your eyes," Steve said.

The team created a proposal for a panoramic camera to send to Mars on the Pathfinder mission. But Steve and his team made a mistake in their calculations. The proposed camera wouldn't fit in the proposed spacecraft, and the National Aeronautics and Space Administration (NASA) turned them down.

So Steve aimed for the next Mars mission, in 1998. He and his team proposed all kinds of cool equipment, including the panoramic camera; another camera that would look down as the spacecraft landed; a spectrometer that would help the team figure out what was in the soil; a close-up camera; and a tool for measuring the weather. The proposal seemed airtight, and Steve thought they had it in the bag. But NASA turned down this one, too.

Steve kept returning to the idea of sending a geologist to Mars. But the goal seemed impossible. Mars is tens of millions of miles away. It would take a spacecraft six months to get there.

Mars is an extremely harsh planet. It's bitterly cold. The average temperature is 75 degrees *below*

The Viking landers couldn't walk across the Martian surface. "Imagine you're a geologist and you get sent out to some cool place you've never been," Steve explained. "They helicopter you in and set you down and say, 'We'll pick you up in a day.' And then they *nail down your boots* so you can't walk around. The story is there to be read in the rocks but you can't reach it."

Gazing at the Viking photos, Steve longed to wander around the red planet, to scratch away the dust, to get beneath the rocks and soil. "I walked out of that room knowing exactly what I wanted to do with the rest of my life," he said.

• • •

"I walked out of that room knowing exactly what I wanted to do with the rest of my life."

zero Fahrenheit. Martian summers feature wicked windstorms and winters are dark and frigid. The planet is arid and airless, and is constantly bombarded by deadly radiation. Just packing adequate supplies to keep someone alive for the trip out would make the mission impossible.

Steve thought, *What if the geologist didn't need food, water, or oxygen? What if the geologist didn't even need somewhere to live or protection from radiation?*

"I imagined sending a robot to Mars, a rolling geologist, with the hammers and drills and tools of a human geologist," he said. A rover could tell so much about Mars and about the possibility of life in other places in the universe.

Steve and his team decided to go big—to propose not just some tools to send to Mars but rather a whole Mars mission, complete with rocket, spacecraft, rover, and instruments.

His idea was a tough sell. "Rovers are risky. They are expensive and difficult to do," he admitted. "And people kept asking, Why do you need a rover when all the rocks on Mars look alike? But all you had to do was look at pictures from orbit and it was obvious that Mars is an incredibly scenic, diverse, and complicated planet."

For eight years, Steve wrote proposals to NASA for a Mars rover.

For eight years, NASA refused to fund the proposals.

But Steve never gave up.

"I'm stubborn," he said, "and stubbornness pays off."

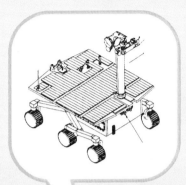

This is Steve's original vision for a rover he wanted to send to Mars.

Steve Squyres made many presentations on his ideas for a Mars rover. He is pictured here in a meeting at NASA headquarters.

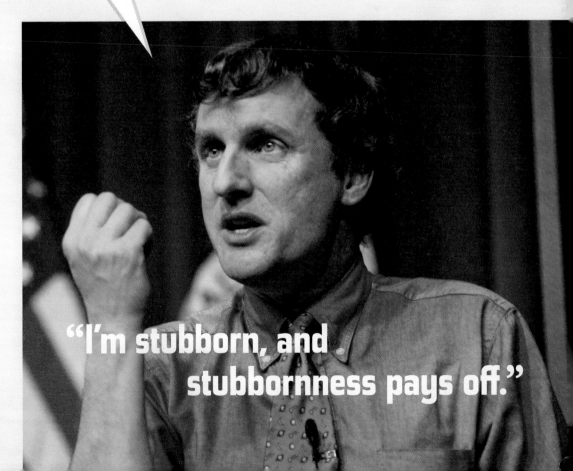

"I'm stubborn, and stubbornness pays off."

2 The Making of the Mars Rovers

In 2000, Steve got a surprising call from NASA.

"Can you build two?"

"Two what?" Steve asked.

NASA wanted two rockets, two landers, two rovers, two of everything. The two Mars Exploration Rovers would be identical but would land on opposite sides of the planet. Having two of them, NASA hoped, would double the chances of success—success that was needed dearly after a string of mission failures.

Steve jumped at the chance.

Launches to Mars are planned during an "opposition," when the sun, Earth, and Mars are in alignment. In 2003, Mars's elliptical orbit moved it closer to Earth than it had been in 60,000 years—about 190 million miles closer than normal. It also moved Mars to its closest point to the sun. Meanwhile, Earth was heading toward its farthest point from the sun, meaning it was pushing outward to Mars. This rare coincidence of events brought Earth and Mars extraordinarily close, a perfect circumstance for launching rovers.

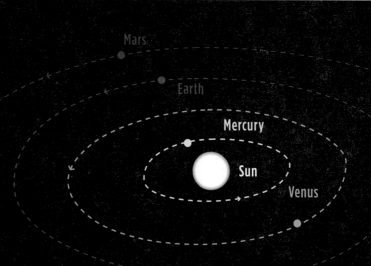

"Our schedule was impossible."

Steve, with his team of 170 scientists, worked with Pete Theisinger and his hundreds of engineers at the Jet Propulsion Laboratory (JPL) in Pasadena, California, to pull together dozens of design-and-build groups. They had to move fast. Launch windows to send spacecraft to Mars come only every twenty-six months. In 2003, Mars's orbit would bring it closer to Earth than usual. The shorter distance would mean better communication. The shorter trip would require less fuel. Mars would also be closer to the sun, offering decent solar power to run the rovers. If Steve missed this opportunity, he wouldn't have one this good for another eighteen years—and NASA wouldn't wait that long.

Steve's and Pete's teams would have three years to complete what mission planners usually completed in five. "Our schedule was almost impossible," Steve said. "It wasn't clear we could even make it to the launch pad, let alone get things

Before entering the "clean room" at the Jet Propulsion Laboratory where the rovers were to be built, engineers had to take an "air shower" that blasted off dirt and dust particles and then suit up head to toe.

to work on Mars. We made a whole bunch of promises . . . Delivering on them now was going to be a struggle."

The scientists had many decisions to make: What would the rovers look like? How would they land on Mars? How would they be powered? How would they move? What instruments would they carry?

Designing and building the rovers involved universities and laboratories all over the country and all over the world. Cables would be built in Colorado, sensors in Germany, magnets in Denmark, and hundreds of thousands of other pieces in other places.

Steve and Pete considered how each decision would affect every other. For example, the scientists wanted to put as many instruments on the rover as possible: cameras, microscopes, drills, and a weather station. Engineers had to design solar panels large enough to power all the instruments. But if the rover got too big, it wouldn't fit in the lander (the case that would protect the rover during landing). Even worse, if the rover and the lander got too heavy, the whole spacecraft would crash.

Steve and his team added instruments and cut instruments. Engineers redesigned solar panels again and again. As the parts were built, engineers tested them. Too often, parts failed. Electronics malfunctioned. Cable cutters designed to set the rovers free from their landers didn't work properly. Parachutes responsible for slowing the rovers down as they careened toward the surface fluttered in the wind and ripped to shreds. Airbags that were supposed to cushion the fall of the rovers onto the surface of Mars tore.

If the parts didn't work, how would the team ever get the rovers to work?

• • •

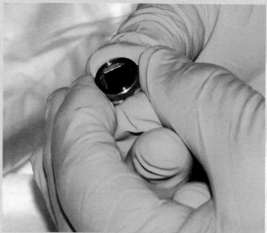

TOP LEFT:
The alpha particle x-ray spectrometer (APXS), built by engineers from Germany's Max Planck Institute, was placed on each rover's arm, where it would help determine the chemical makeup of rocks and soil on Mars.

TOP RIGHT:
This computer chip, holding 35,000 laser-engraved signatures, will travel with one of the rovers to Mars.

CENTER LEFT:
Engineers test a landing parachute in the longest wind tunnel in the world at NASA's Ames Research Center.

CENTER RIGHT:
An obstacle course dubbed the "rock gauntlet" challenged test wheels to scale everything from small rocks to concrete blocks.

BOTTOM:
Pete Theisinger took Steve's dreams and turned them into thousands of parts, which his engineering team would assemble to make the Mars rovers.

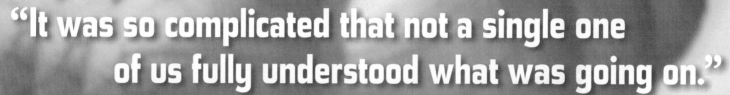

"It was so complicated that not a single one of us fully understood what was going on."

Rob Manning, Entry, Descent and Landing lead, discusses the airbags that would be used in landing the rovers. Each rover will use four airbags with six lobes each, which are all connected. The fabric of the airbags is not attached directly to the rovers. Instead, ropes crisscross the bags and hold the bags to the rover like a net.

The making of the Mars rovers seemed more real to Steve when he visited JPL and suited up for the clean room.

In the shadow of the San Bernardino Mountains in Pasadena, past a mission-style high school and a horse-riding club, Steve showed his badge at the security checkpoint of the Jet Propulsion Laboratory. Less than a year before launch, finished rover pieces began to show up at JPL for ATLO: Assembly, Test, and Launch Operations. Engineers and mechanics worked around the clock to put the pieces together. And Steve wanted to be there to see it happen.

"I love the process of creation and being part of such an extraordinary team, the sense of shared struggle as we pulled together this incredible mission," Steve said. "It was so complicated that not a single one of us fully understood what was going on. But somehow as a group we understood it completely."

In a "clean room," wearing head-to-toe white clean suits, mouth masks, and blue booties, engineers assembled the rovers. As they built, they tested. If something didn't work, they went back, redesigned, rebuilt, and retested.

The rovers begin to come together at JPL.

Steve and his team ran many field tests with a small-scale rover called FIDO (Field Integrated Design and Operations). Here Steve is testing rover mobility in the Mojave Desert.

RAT was not a furry gray creature, but a rock abrasion tool, a drill to bore holes into soil and rock. Then there was the microscopic imager (MI), a cross between a camera and a microscope, which would take extremely up-close photos of rocks and soil. By measuring radiation, the alpha particle x-ray spectrometer (APXS) could identify many elements and the Mössbauer spectrometer could detect iron-bearing minerals in the rocks and soil.

Flat panels spread out from each side of the rovers like butterfly wings. These solar panels absorbed sunlight and converted it to electricity. Just like us, the rovers would be "awake" in the day and "asleep" at night to conserve energy. The rovers had batteries, but they could store only so much power. This was the rovers' greatest weakness.

"Sun is just so important to the lives of these rovers," said Steve. "Without daily sunlight, the rovers would freeze solid."

Steve couldn't believe that the team had actually managed to build the rovers in just

"After all the years of hope and planning, seeing our rovers start to become real was deeply moving."

Steve spent days and nights at JPL overseeing the science instruments and watching assembly of the rest of the rover. "After all the years of hope and planning, seeing our rovers start to become real was deeply moving," he said.

Little by little, the rovers began to resemble six-legged animals, but instead of legs, they had six wheels that could move independently of one another. Instead of tails, they had rear antennae. Their small robotlike heads pivoted on long pipe necks. Right where eyes would go were two navigation cameras, called Navcams, that would work like eyeballs, scanning the ground before them, showing what lay ahead. The little robots had another set of "eyes" on their head: two panoramic cameras, called Pancams, that would take photos of the vast Martian landscape.

Each robot had one arm with an elbow that held all kinds of cool gadgets, like the RAT. The

Engineers install solar panels in JPL's Spacecraft Assembly Facility.

Nine-year-old Sofi Collis with her adoptive American family.

What's in a Name?

Your parents named you, but who named the Mars rovers? NASA held a contest, and Sofi Collis, a nine-year-old girl born in Siberia who was adopted by a family in Arizona, won with the names Spirit and Opportunity. This is what she wrote in her essay:

I used to live in an orphanage. It was dark and cold and lonely. At night, I looked up at the sparkly sky and felt better. I dreamed I could fly there. In America, I can make all my dreams come true. Thank you for the "Spirit" and the "Opportunity."

"The first time I saw Spirit move, it brought tears to my eyes."

Members of the Mars Exploration Rover team watch closely as Spirit rolls over a ramp in the high bay floor.

three years. NASA named them "Spirit" and "Opportunity."

"I do my best to play the big, steely-eyed space explorer dude," said Steve. "But the first time I saw Spirit move, crawling slowly forward over blue plastic mats on the high bay floor, it brought tears to my eyes."

Even after the rovers were fully assembled, testing continued. Spirit failed test after test. Her camera took speckled photos. Her transmitters didn't send messages properly. Her arm joint short-circuited. Engineers fixed all the problems they could find on both rovers. Opportunity passed his tests with flying colors.

But did the engineers miss anything? Steve's and Pete's teams had no more time to find out.

The rovers were scheduled to be rocketed separately to different parts of Mars. And it was time for Spirit to launch.

"We had done our best to prepare her for the dangers she would face, but had we done enough?"

Five . . . four . . . three

On June 10, 2003, riding on a *Delta 2* rocket, Spirit blasted off from Cape Canaveral, Florida, with a blinding explosion of light and billowing steam. Steve craned his neck to watch the white-tipped rocket rise toward space. As Spirit headed for Mars, team members around the world hugged one another. "We had done our best to prepare her for the dangers she would face, but had we done enough?" Steve wondered. "We would hear from her in the months ahead, reading her temperatures and her voltages, and viewing her pictures—if she made it safely to Mars. But none of us would ever see her again with our own eyes, and that made me surprisingly sad. It was hard to let go."

On July 7, less than a month after Spirit was launched, Opportunity soared through the solar system hot on her trail. Millions of people, not just the mission scientists and engineers, crossed their fingers for a safe trip.

The flight would take about six months, and no one knew how the rovers would fare. Steve did what he always does during the scariest stages of a mission: he wore his good-luck necklace, with the tip of a reindeer antler. "I'm embarrassed to admit it, but I'm terribly superstitious about space missions," he said. "Yes, I know, it's utterly illogical. There's no way that what you wear can have any effect on a piece of hardware hundreds of millions of miles out in space."

The *Delta 2* rocket with Mars rover Spirit aboard leaps off the launch pad into the blue sky. Liftoff occurred at 1:58 p.m. Eastern Daylight Time on June 10, 2003, from Cape Canaveral Air Force Station in Florida.

... two ... one!

Trouble started just a few months into the journey to Mars. Spirit and Opportunity were blasted with big bursts of solar radiation. Solar flares are normal, but these were the strongest flares ever recorded. What if the radiation messed with the electronics? What if an important electronic component broke? Everything onboard was precisely engineered. What if something sent the rovers off course?

As the spacecrafts continued their six-month flights, bad news from other Mars missions poured in. A month before the rovers were due to land on the red planet, Japan's Mars orbiter *Nozomi*, which means "hope," was lost in space. Days later the British Mars lander *Beagle 2* disappeared.

As Spirit and Opportunity neared Mars, TV and newspaper reporters, scientists and engineers, and space enthusiasts around the world watched and worried.

Opportunity's launch was postponed more than half a dozen times because of bad weather, a failed battery cell, and problems with insulation. The nighttime launch at 11:18 p.m. on July 7, 2003, momentarily illuminated Florida coast beaches.

3 Are We Really on Mars?

As expected, Spirit approached the Martian atmosphere first. She had made it this far, but landing on Mars would be tricky, requiring split-second timing. Many things could go wrong, fatally wrong. If the lander didn't pass through the atmosphere just right, it would burn up from friction. A parachute and retrorockets were supposed to slow the rover's screaming descent, but if they didn't deploy, the spacecraft would be smashed to a million pieces. The final stage of landing would be free fall, from 30 feet (9 m) in the air, protected only by a cushion of airbags that encircled the robot. Even if all went well, Spirit would bounce like a superball—as much as six stories high—time and time again. Finally she would roll to a stop, but no one knew where or in what condition.

The entry, descent, and landing (EDL) phase begins when the spacecraft reaches the Mars atmospheric entry point, about 2,113 miles (3522.2 km) from the center of Mars.

Steve Squyres and his team knew that the landing would take about six minutes. They also knew that radio signals from Mars take ten minutes to reach Earth. This meant that for ten minutes of terror, scientists couldn't correct anything that went wrong. "We would be helpless," Steve said. "Watching . . . waiting . . ."

In the large room at the Jet Propulsion Laboratory that served as Mission Control for the landing, rows of computers made a semicircle around wide screens and people packed in where they could find room. For good luck, all the scientists and engineers at Mission Control munched peanuts, because once when someone had brought peanuts to share during a landing, all had gone well. "I tore mine open and began to munch immediately, the one and only thing I could do to improve our chances of a safe landing," said Steve.

The six-minute landing began. Scientists hoped that Spirit would separate from her rocket properly. They worried about her burning through the Martian sky at twenty-five times the speed of sound. They prayed that the parachute and retrorockets would do their jobs as Spirit plummeted toward the ground. And they hoped that the precious little rover, wrapped in its cocoon of airbags, would survive all the bouncing.

"We would be helpless. Watching . . . waiting . . ."

Mark Adler (blue shirt), deputy director of the Mars Exploration Rover project, and other team members in Mission Control at NASA's Jet Propulsion Laboratory in Pasadena, California, awaiting the landing of Spirit on the surface of Mars.

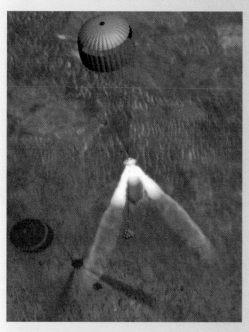

To slow the lander's speed, retrorockets fire. Airbags inflate to cushion the fall.

Communications during entry, descent, and landing occur through a pair of antennas, one mounted on the backshell and the other on the rover itself, wrapped in its cushion of airbags. About 36 ten-second radio tones are transmitted to Earth during descent, coded to indicate the accomplishment of critical steps.

The first announcement came over a loudspeaker from the landing manager, who handled the transition from flight operations to surface operations.

The room became hushed.

"We have a signal indicating bouncing on the surface."

Mission Control exploded with hugs, cheers, and tears. Steve pounded his fists on the tabletop, eyes pressed tightly closed. *Are we really on Mars?*

Then everything stopped.

The signal was lost.

The room went silent again.

A long minute.

The flight team reestablished contact. "We see it! We see it! We see it!"

Then the words Steve had been waiting for from the flight team: "Surface, Flight. Spirit is yours."

Spirit shook off her airbags and stretched her solar wings to charge her batteries. The scientists couldn't wait for her to start snapping pictures. From Mars orbiter photos, Gusev Crater, her landing spot, appeared to be a ninety-five-mile-wide lakebed with a river channel feeding into it. Scientists thought Gusev was their best shot at finding signs of water.

And there on the screen was the first image from Mars.

"Oh my God!" Steve gasped.

The colors were so perfect, and the details so sharp, it was like being there. "It works, man ... It works," he muttered.

"It works, man . . . it works."

Steve Squyres, center, reacts as NASA administrator Sean O'Keefe, left, looks on as they get a signal from the Mars rover Spirit after she landed.

The first 360-degree view of the Martian surface, taken by Spirit's panoramic camera, or Pancam.

The red, rocky expanse resembled the Mojave Desert, with windblown dust and small, dark rocks casting shadows in the afternoon sun. The area was flat, with no big boulders or hills.

Could this be what a Martian lakebed looked like up close?

Scientists wouldn't learn more until Spirit, the mobile geologist, started driving, digging, poking, and analyzing the dust and rocks. It took days to maneuver Spirit off her landing pad. Then the rover drivers directed Spirit toward a small pyramid-shaped rock, which the scientists called Adirondack, about 10 feet (3 m) straight ahead.

This is more complicated than it sounds. Signals from the rover, such as a photo of a dangerous ditch in her path, took ten minutes to reach Earth. Commands back to the rover, like "STOP!," took another ten minutes. Driving a rover is not like playing a video game—you can't just move your joystick and watch the rover obey. Instead, rover drivers carefully study the terrain ahead of time so they can safely map out the rovers' moves. Roughly once a day, the team gets photos of the rover's surroundings, and about once a day, they send commands that tell the rover what to do.

Spirit crept along, with her drivers correcting her direction daily. It took three days, but finally she pointed her tools directly at the rock.

Would she find signs of water?

Peter T. Poon, telecommunications and mission systems manager for JPL, looks at a 3-D panorama image taken by Spirit.

"Are we really on Mars?"

Naming Names

When Steve and his team talked about what the rovers saw around them on Mars, they couldn't just say "that crater" or "this rock" or "those hills." It would be too confusing. The International Astronomical Union (IAU) is responsible for naming land features on planets other than Earth. But the team had to discuss what the rovers should do daily, so they couldn't wait. Jim Rice, a geologist at Arizona State University and a rover science-team member, suggested that features studied on the mission be temporarily named according to themes. "OK," Steve said. "You're in charge."

The team decided to name craters near Spirit's landing site after lakes on Earth (Bonneville, for instance). Craters near Opportunity's landing site would be named after famous ships of exploration, hence Eagle (the *Apollo 11* lunar lander) and Endurance (after Ernest Shackleton's Antarctic expedition). The Columbia Hills were named after the space shuttle *Columbia,* and each of the seven peaks were named after the lost *Columbia* astronauts.

But there were so many features to name that soon the rules fell apart. Basically whoever started studying a rock or hill or crater got to name it. So there are place names (Adirondack and Stone Mountain), people names (Burns Cliff and Larry's Leap), and even foods (Mudpie, Chocolate Chip, and Cookies and Cream).

"Whenever explorers go somewhere, we always want to name things," says Jim Rice. "It's just something we humans like to do."

Adirondack, Spirit's first target rock, selected because its dust-free, flat surface was perfect for grinding. Spirit traversed the sandy Martian terrain at Gusev Crater to arrive in front of the football-size rock just three days after the rover successfully rolled off the lander. Scientists named the angular rock after the Adirondack mountain range in New York.

Rover driver Scott Maxwell on his first rover drive: "That night, I lay in bed looking up at the ceiling and thinking that right at that moment there was a robot on another planet doing what I told it to do. That was an incredible thrill. That feeling has never left me, when I'm about make something happen on my computer. I'm going to reach my hand across a hundred million miles of empty space and move something on the surface of another world. I have the coolest job."

How to Drive a Rover

Rover driver Scott Maxwell sat down at his computer and called up an image of Mars. But the image didn't look like a photo. It had the sharp angles and flat, bold colors of a video game. Using his mouse, Scott started to move the scene around. The sky was a dusty butterscotch color—as it is on Mars. The beige areas were parts of the scene the rover couldn't see because its body got in the way. "We can spin it around," Scott said—the photo whirls—"zoom in on things that are interesting"—a rock grows large on the screen— "even mark off areas that we think are dangerous"—Scott drew red circles around two large rocks and a small crater. He clicked a rover into the middle of the scene and moved it around. "Now we can sketch out a path that we want the rover to drive along," he added.

It looks fun—and easy—but it's not so simple. The rover drivers test the maneuvers many times before sending drive commands to the rovers. "Part of the game is figuring out what things could possibly go wrong," said Scott. "If something goes wrong and you break the rovers, there is no way to fix them."

"We haven't heard anything from the spacecraft all day," Jennifer Trosper, the mission manager, told Steve the day they were set to RAT the rock. They kept trying.

"Earth to Spirit."

Silence.

"Earth to Spirit. Come in, Spirit!"

Lead engineer Pete Theisinger called all the mission managers and flight directors on the team into the conference room. Ideas flew. Maybe Spirit had shut herself down to cool off. Maybe her batteries were too low. Maybe the software had failed. Steve held on to one hope: maybe Spirit would phone home the next day as if nothing had gone wrong.

The whole team was there the next day when Spirit was scheduled to send a signal. "We've got data!"

Steve phoned his wife. "We got it," he said, his voice cracking.

But too soon the cheering died down and the smiles faded. Spirit transmitted gibberish for two minutes and then shut off.

"It hit me then," Steve said. "The whole mission could be over before it ever really began."

While Spirit's engineers struggled to fix the ailing rover, another team of engineers was guiding her twin, Opportunity, toward his fiery landing on the red planet. They all knew that if Spirit couldn't communicate and Opportunity crashed, all would be lost.

The mission would be a complete failure.

Another tense moment at Mission Control.

Communications specialist Serjik Zadourian checks with antenna stations around the world to listen for a signal from Spirit.

"The whole mission could be over before it ever really began."

Chatting with the Rovers

In this story, the scientist and rovers seem to speak to each other using words. But scientists can't really "talk" to the rovers. To communicate, scientists type codes and commands that they beam to one of three huge satellite dishes in Earth's Deep Space Network (DSN). The dish passes the commands to a spacecraft that is orbiting Mars, usually the *Mars Odyssey,* which beams them to the rovers at an appointed time.

"You get a beep from the rover that means 'Thank you, I got my commands.' Then you don't hear from it for the rest of the day," said Matt Golombek, who manages rover planning. "You can't watch the rover; you can't listen to it. You really have no idea what is happening."

The team hopes the rovers follow the commands, driving, taking photos, and testing and measuring rocks. At a scheduled time, the rovers radiate the information they have gathered to *Odyssey* via their low-gain UHF antennas. *Odyssey,* directed to listen at that time, collects the signals. Sometime later, it downlinks the data to JPL through the Deep Space Network.

The rovers can phone home directly to Earth using their high-gain antennas, but they don't have to "yell" as loudly or use as much energy if they send messages through the orbiter. And they can send bigger messages, faster. That pleases the scientists who are eager for their rovers to phone home.

Matt Golombek awaits information on Opportunity's previous day's work at a science planning meeting.

Dawn shot of an antenna at the Goldstone Deep Space Communications Complex, located in the Mojave Desert in California, one of three complexes in NASA's Deep Space Network (DSN). The DSN provides radio communications for all of NASA's interplanetary spacecraft, including the rovers.

"I'm sorry, I'm just—I'm blown away by this."

Opportunity neared the red planet. *Crack!* Off came his rocket. Opportunity burned through the Martian sky. *Whoosh!* His parachute ballooned. *Roar!* His retrorockets thrust against gravity. Airbags deployed! Free fall! BOUNCE…way up high…BOUNCE…high to the sky again…BOUNCE…plummeting down and rebounding up again…BOUNCE…and again…BOUNCE…and again! Opportunity bounced about twenty-six times before rolling to a halt.

"BEEP!" Opportunity signaled that he had landed.

Mission Control erupted into cheers.

The team was thrilled. But they expected to find less at Opportunity's landing site than they had found at Spirit's. Scientists had chosen Meridiani Planum because it was the safest area to land, flat and featureless. Opportunity would probably have to drive around for a while over the fine red soil, they thought, to even find a rock worth studying.

Opportunity shook off his airbags, unfolded his instruments, and beamed his first photos to Mission Control.

"Holy smokes!" Steve Squyres exclaimed. "I'm sorry, I'm just—I'm blown away by this."

Just 10 yards away, large, layered slabs of rock jutted out in front of the rover. Opportunity had landed smack in a shallow crater, about 30 yards wide and a couple of yards deep. It was like scoring a great big interplanetary hole in one!

Steve Squyres celebrates with others in Mission Control at the successful landing of the second rover, Opportunity.

This computer-generated red line shows Opportunity's bounces as the rover landed at Meridiani Planum. The spacecraft bounced north approximately twenty-six times while safely encased in airbags, until it came to a stop inside a crater.

More pictures flashed on the screen. Opportunity's photos showed exposed rock layers that scientists had never before seen on Mars.

Steve's eyes widened. "That outcrop in the distance is just out of this world. I can't wait to get there. I've got nothing else to say. I just want to look."

Somebody called out, "Did we hit the sweet spot?"

"This is the sweetest spot I've ever seen!" is all Steve could manage in reply.

Why was Steve so thrilled to see rock layers? On Earth and on Mars, rock layers tell us about the geologic, weather, and climate conditions that prevailed during the years and decades each layer was formed. It's like rings inside a tree stump: some rings are thick and others are thin, reflecting the weather conditions that accompanied the tree's growth. Steve and the other scientists looked at rock layers the rover photographed and wondered whether they were brought about by volcanic eruptions, blowing dust, flowing water, or all three.

Over the coming days and weeks, Steve and his team studied the images that filled their screens, and debated what they meant. Many of Opportunity's photos featured blueberry-shaped pebbles strewn across the soil, like beads spilled from a broken necklace. "They were the strangest-looking things I'd ever seen on Mars," said Steve.

Some team members thought the pebbles looked like volcanic hailstones. Others thought they might be droplets of lava that had cooled quickly.

Like detectives intent on understanding a clue, the team considered other possibilities. Maybe the rocks had rolled around in *water*, which smoothed them. Maybe material dissolved in *water* had dried out and solidified layer by layer to make the round forms. Was what they were seeing evidence that water had once existed on Mars?

To find out, Opportunity took close-up photos, tried RATing a blueberry, and took measurements with his APXS and Mössbauer. He discovered some salts!

Hmm, thought Steve and his colleagues. Salts are often left behind when water evaporates. But some team members needed more to convince them.

Opportunity kept exploring.

"We treated the rovers very carefully," said rover driver Scott Maxwell. "We didn't want to make them do things like drive over rocks, for fear of breaking them." Even so, discoveries poured in. Opportunity found jarosite—a kind of salt that on Earth forms in the presence of water, in acidic lakes or hot springs. Still, the scientists didn't want to jump to conclusions – maybe things are different on Mars?

The team pondered photos of ridges in the rocks. They looked just like ripples in the sand made by ocean waves on planet Earth.

As the clues poured in, Steve and the other scientists became convinced.

"Evidence pointed again and again to the existence at some time of a flowing, salty body of water on Mars," said Steve. "It was undeniable!"

Just weeks after landing, Opportunity had found evidence that water once pooled on the surface of this area of Mars. "We landed and *boom*,

This 3-D topographic map shows Opportunity's landing site, Eagle Crater, estimated to be 9.8 feet (3 m) deep and 72.2 feet (22 m) across.

This high-resolution image captured by Opportunity's panoramic camera shows the rock outcrop on the rim of Eagle Crater, where the rover landed. These layered rocks measure only 4 inches (10 cm) high. Data from the panoramic camera's near-infrared blue and green filters were combined to create this approximate, true-color image.

there it was, handed to us on a silver platter. We couldn't believe our luck," Steve said.

But important questions remained: Had the water been warm enough and deep enough, and had it been there long enough, for life to form?

Steve Squyres shares the amazing discoveries from Opportunity's latest images of bedrock in Eagle Crater.

This magnified photo of Eagle Crater, taken by the Microscopic Imager on Opportunity's arm, shows coarse grains that scientists nicknamed blueberries. The examined patch of soil is 1.2 inches (3 cm) across, and the largest blueberry shown is about the size of a sunflower seed.

"They were the strangest-looking things I'd ever seen on Mars."

4 Hitting the Dusty Trail

Meanwhile, Spirit's team kept receiving short spurts of data, which they analyzed furiously. They didn't understand why they couldn't communicate better with Spirit. Why did her computer keep rebooting?

"Okay, so what are the top theories?" asked Matt Wallace, one of the mission's engineering leaders.

"We don't have enough data to have any top theories," a team member said, opening up his laptop to show a table that listed what had happened and what they knew for certain. There was very little they knew for certain.

Then the situation worsened.

Spirit was not shutting down properly at night to conserve energy. Her battery was extremely low. "We've got to get her to shut down hard and let the power system get healthy again," Pete Theisinger told the team. Steve agreed.

So they sent a command that they had used in the testing phase when things went haywire and they wanted to start over. "SHUTDOWN_DAMMIT" had never failed them before.

Sleep deprived, Steve thought he should get some shuteye, too. He was in the parking lot heading to his car when he ran into Pete.

"Did you hear?" Pete asked.

Steve stopped in his tracks. "Hear what?"

"[Spirit] woke up again."

"What?" Steve wheeled around and headed back toward the building. Spirit stayed awake all night, draining her battery, crashing and rebooting over and over.

Glenn Reeves, one of the architects of Spirit's software, pored over what little data they managed to get from Spirit. He noticed that Spirit sent only the data she had collected in the most recent two minutes. There was nothing from even five minutes earlier. Where was the data that should have been in Spirit's flash memory? Perhaps the flash wasn't working properly.

The team quickly tested Glenn's theory. They sent a command to restart Spirit's system without using the flash memory. The system restarted.

So they shut down the rover and gave her some time so the sun could fully recharge her batteries. Then they downloaded software to fix the flash.

Jennifer Trosper, mission manager for surface operations, and Steve Squyres celebrate Spirit's early successes at a press conference.

It worked. On a whiteboard in the office someone scrawled: "The Spirit was willing, but the flash was weak."

Spirit was finally ready to start her quest for signs of water.

Spirit makes tracks near her landing spot.

• • •

Spirit scooted off, taking photos and prodding rocks. From orbiter photos, Gusev Crater, Spirit's landing spot, looked like it was once a lake. Steve and the rest of the team couldn't wait to see what the little rover would find.

Using her mini-TES (miniature thermal emission spectrometer), Spirit scanned rocks in the distance to see if there was anything interesting in their composition. To Steve and the other scientists, everything was interesting.

They sent Spirit, ever so carefully, toward a rock. This is what Steve had dreamed would happen! Spirit snapped a photo. She reached her arm toward the rock. With her microscopic imager, Spirit snapped close-ups. She measured chemicals with her alpha particle x-ray spectrometer. She drilled holes, snapped more pictures, and took more measurements.

Guess what she found?

Not much. Nothing but basalt, a common form of lava.

There were no minerals or other clues that the basalt had been altered by water.

Spirit searched and searched. She scooted around Gusev, scanning, measuring, drilling, and remeasuring. She photographed rocks, brushed rocks, drilled rocks, and measured rocks.

Each time Spirit approached a rock, the team was hopeful. "We hit it with all the tools we had," Steve said. "In the end, though, we knew what we would find: a chunk of basalt with a coating of dust on the outside."

Was it possible, the team wondered, that water had once covered the area but lava from a volcanic eruption had covered up all the evidence?

It was March, nearly three months into what the team had projected would be a three-month mission. No one would have been surprised if the rover broke, lost power, or just lost touch. Steve hoped they could get another three months' work out of Spirit. Her team huddled up to decide what to do next.

Some team members suggested facing facts.

There were no signs of water anywhere nearby. Maybe they should focus on learning more about Martian lava. Others suggested looking somewhere else. But where?

Steve was itching for a discovery.

Off in the distance, some hills rose up. Perhaps they were high enough to be above the lava flow. "How about the Columbia Hills?" someone joked. Everyone laughed. The line of hills was a mile and a half away—more than four times Spirit's expected travel distance of a third of a mile (600 m).

Plus, the hills were some 300 feet high (91 meters) and looked crumbly, boulder-strewn, and steep. The rovers had been designed to cruise flat plains. No one expected that Spirit could climb hills like those.

"But the hills are the only things for miles around in any direction that are potentially different from what we've seen so far," Steve argued to his team. "Maybe we can get to the base of the hills and take a quick look before winter hits and the rover dies."

Spirit's front hazard identification camera captures the robotic arm at work, extending toward Adirondack to identify its mineral composition.

"We hit it with all the tools we had."

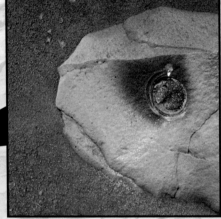

During the first grinding of a rock on Mars, the rock abrasion tool on Spirit ground off 0.1 inch (0.65 mm) of a surface of Adirondack that was 1.8 inches (45.5 mm) wide, exposing fresh interior material of the rock for close inspection.

This traverse map traces the path Spirit drove toward a crater called Bonneville during its original mission of 90 sols, or Martian days.

This picture is a simulation of Spirit at the rim of the Bonneville Crater. Spirit did not descend into the crater because it was filled with what looked like soft dust.

100 m

Lava, lava everywhere!

This image shows the Martian terrain through the eyes of Spirit's mini-TES, an instrument that detects the infrared light, or heat, emitted by soil and rocks. The color red represents warmer regions and blue, cooler. Scientists use this image to pinpoint features of interest and to plot a safe course for the rover around areas with loose dust.

Master watchmaker Garo Anserlian of Executive Jewelers made the perfect timepiece for the Mars rovers team members. The watches lose 39 minutes a day. "I felt proud," Garo said after the two rovers landed safely. "I got goose bumps. I saw that some of [the mission scientists] had two watches on and I thought, *One of them is mine!*"

Living on Martian Time

Mars has four seasons, like Earth, but a Martian year lasts almost twice as long (687 days) as an Earth year, so Martian seasons are twice as long, too.

A Martian day, called a sol, is twenty-four hours, thirty-nine minutes, and thirty-five seconds long. The extra forty minutes or so, compared to an Earth day, may not seem like much. But the rovers communicated with the orbiters at the same time once every Martian day. So the meetings to review the day's photos and data and plan the rovers' activities for the next day were scheduled based on Martian time.

A meeting might start out at a reasonable hour for Earthlings. But for the team to stay on Martian time, the next day's meeting had to begin thirty-nine minutes later. In three weeks, the team was meeting in the middle of the night!

With the two rovers operating in two Martian time zones, twelve hours apart, team members who were working on both rovers suffered major jet lag each time they switched from one rover to the other. Steve and his team members started wearing two watches, one set to Earth time and the other to Mars time. They also created their own language to deal with living on Martian time: they had "Spirit sols" and "Opportunity sols" to mark the rovers' Martian days, and even "yestersol" to refer to the previous day on Mars.

"There is a very good chance we won't make it."

If Spirit traveled 197 feet (60 m) each Martian day, or sol, Steve and his team calculated, the journey of 1.7 miles (2.7 km) to the Columbia Hills would take her forty-five days to complete. Add in some time to take measurements along the way, and the team estimated it would be two months before the rover reached the hills. That would be two months past her expected survival time.

"There's a very good chance that we won't make it," Steve admitted.

But the team decided to go for it anyway.

Opportunity's team met, too, in the Science Operations Working Group (SOWG) room, with its large screens, black walls, and blackout curtains. Faces of scientists from around the country flashed up onscreen as the team debated plans for what they thought would be the last few months of Opportunity's mission.

Eagle Crater, where Opportunity had landed, was amazing, but a bigger crater might give an even richer picture of the history of water on Mars. Team members rolled out an image strip, a long photo 3 feet wide and 20 feet long (1 m by 6 m), to get a good look at Opportunity's surroundings.

Eagle Crater was at one end of the strip. Far off on the other side of the strip was Endurance Crater, more than a half mile (800 m) away. Like Spirit, Opportunity was expected to travel only a third of a mile (600 m) during his entire mission. With the slow, careful driving required to keep Opportunity from crashing, the trip would take at least six weeks, longer than the rover's life expectancy.

"It's clearly outside our design parameters. It's not a slam dunk," said Steve, "but boy, Endurance looks cool." So the team made the most audacious decision possible. Opportunity would head for Endurance.

Off both rovers went.

Across the planet from each other, the two rovers had very different trips. Opportunity faced a flat expanse of sand and smooth rock. "We just pushed the pedal down and let [him] go," Steve said. "Like you're driving across a giant parking lot."

The journey was much harder for Spirit. "Spirit's site was so littered with rocks and boulders," Steve said sadly. "That's tough on a machine."

As Spirit neared the Columbia Hills, bumps and boulders blocked her path. Unlike the hard lava, these rocks seemed soft, almost chalky—even rotted and crumbly.

For weeks, as Spirit picked her way through the boulder-strewn plains, her photos looked the same. Then things started to change. As Spirit neared the hills, they seemed to loom higher and higher in the photos. The scientists could make out slopes, peaks, and valleys. Rocky outcrops came into view a little way up the slopes. Spirit had already gone three times farther than the scientists thought she would go and had lived longer than she was supposed to live. Reaching the base of the Columbia Hills was a great accomplishment.

And while Spirit continued to search the base of the hills, her twin across the planet neared the rim of the Endurance Crater.

Driving Without a Driver

The rover drivers mapped out courses for the rovers, but the little machines had to face many obstacles on their own, with no help from the scientists. They depended heavily on their hazard avoidance cameras, or hazcams. At regular intervals, the rovers stopped and took stereo pictures, from two different cameras. Onboard computers built 3-D images of the boulders ahead. The rovers were programmed to avoid driving over anything higher than their wheels. When they approached a rock that exceeded the height of their wheels, they turned away until they got past it. Counting wheel turns and using the sun's place in the sky to determine what direction they were pointed in, they calculated how far off the command path they had wandered and returned to the path on the other side of the obstacle.

5 Can Opportunity Climb Down?

SOL 1 to 3 SOL 56
SOL 48 to 50
SOL 70
SOL 73 to 80
SOL 82
SOL 81
SOL 84
SOL 87
SOL 68 to 69
Anatolia
Fram
(244 m, 126deg)

Eagle Crater

Endurance Center

As of its ninety-first Martian day, Opportunity was about 525 feet (160 m) from the rim of Endurance Crater.

Opportunity's team gazed at the screen, looking at orbital photos of Endurance Crater from the Mars global surveyor to map out their next steps. Team member Mike Malin shook his head in dismay. "The whole thing is going to be so steep that all we'll be able to do is look in from the lip, say, 'Oh, how pretty,' and move on."

Behold Endurance! Perched 15.7 inches (40 cm) away from the edge of Endurance Crater, Opportunity took this panoramic image. The challenge would be getting to the scientific targets: most of the crater's rocks are embedded in steep cliffs.

The team planned for the rover to take a 65-foot (20-m) drive to reach the rim and then to take some pictures. But Opportunity didn't go the distance. He sensed a hazard and stopped short.

The team awaited photos on the screen. Suddenly, there it was laid out before them: Endurance. The crater was bigger than a football stadium and had steep sides and jutting overhangs. Crags and pinnacles dotted the rim. Even the lower slopes were treacherous, steep, and sandy, and were scattered with boulders.

"I couldn't wait to get down there," Steve said. But could Opportunity climb down?

Steve and his team discussed what they knew about rovers and hill climbing. At about 45 degrees, the rover will flip over. Theoretically, Opportunity would be able to roll down anything with a gentler slope.

Getting back up the slope would be the real challenge. When Opportunity had first tried to climb out of Eagle, his landing crater, he'd spun his wheels and gone nowhere. And that slope was only 17 degrees. He managed to get out by zigzagging up. Maybe he would do better here, where the ground looked more solid, but it seemed doubtful.

"So here's the problem," Steve said. "If the gentlest slope we can find anywhere around the rim of Endurance is between 20 and 40 degrees, then this thing could be a permanent rover trap."

Steve Squyres speaks at a press briefing on Opportunity at NASA headquarters in Washington, D.C.

"I couldn't wait to get down there."

If Opportunity went into the crater and couldn't climb back out, that would be the end of his mission.

The scientists stared at photos of layered bedrock on the slopes of the crater. "That's ten times more geologic record than we've been able to see until now," Steve breathed. "If we can work our way down into Endurance Crater, it'll be like traveling back in time."

The scientists and engineers met to debate the worth of the science compared to the risk to the rover. Steve stood in front of a map projected onto a huge screen. He made his case for the knowledge to be gained by descending into the crater, and described a strategy he thought would keep the rover safe. "I would plan to drive only as far down as we need to drive to reach to the lower bound of the exposed bedrock," he said, indicating the spot on a fresh photo from Mars.

Engineer Matt Wallace spoke immediately and decisively. "If we can't climb pretty reliably up these rocks at twenty-five degrees, we are not going into this crater."

The whole team understood the enormity of their decision. If Opportunity went into the crater and couldn't climb back out, that would be the end of his mission. And team members were beginning to feel attached to their little rovers. "Opportunity has to die somewhere," Steve said. "And as I look at Endurance, I can't help thinking that maybe it's the right place to do it."

Engineers drive a test rover to decide whether it would be safe to send Opportunity into Endurance Crater. The slope was so steep that the engineers had to wear a safety harness and rope. The rover, though, was on its own.

So Team Opportunity went shopping. At the Home Depot they bought paving stones, sand, and clay, then hauled it all back to JPL. Engineers constructed a giant sandbox with a huge yellow forklift rigged on one side to tilt the box so it would mimic the Martian slope. Inside the box, they glued smooth paving stones onto plywood and filled the gaps with sand.

When it was ready they would call in a rover identical to the twins, Spirit and Opportunity's triplet, to see whether it could climb the slope.

Steve protested when he saw the test bed. "We can't use that!"

"You mean because it's so smooth?" Matt Wallace asked.

"Of course I mean because it's so smooth! It's *way* too smooth."

They reviewed the photos of the entrance into Endurance. Steve was counting on the rough and lumpy rocks to give the rover's wheels something to grab.

"Okay, look, how about this," Matt proposed. "How about if we bring the rover up here tomorrow and try to run it up the slope, but we just call it an engineering checkout." If the replica rover failed the test, Matt explained, no one would freak out and bar Opportunity from entering Endurance.

Steve agreed, but still he had grave doubts. "I don't think there's any way the rover's going to be able to climb that thing."

"We did it today," Matt told Steve on his cell.

"And?"

"And the thing really scampered up the slope."

Steve watched, mouth agape, as the replica rover's wheels grabbed the rock and rolled up the hill. Most *people* would slip down a slope that steep.

Still, this was just a test; plunging into a crater on Mars could be much more dangerous.

The team made a plan. They would take it

slowly, driving Opportunity in one rover length and then driving out. The next day, they would move a few rover lengths in and then drive back one or two. Two steps forward, one step back.

"We'll work our way slowly downward," Steve suggested. "We'll measure the composition and texture of the rocks in a systematic way, working our way back through the layers of time."

Steve hoped the rough surface of the stones leading into Endurance would give Opportunity enough traction to drive safely in—and out of—the crater. This simulated image superimposed a photo from Mars with a photo of the rover's wheels.

Opportunity's scientists crossed their fingers as they commanded the rover over the rim.

The team gathered quietly around the consoles the next day, waiting for the data, waiting for photos. The silence was unnerving for Steve.

Then the data started to hit.

"Tilt is nine degrees," said one of the engineers. That was pretty flat, indicating that Opportunity had to be off the steep slope—if he had actually gone into the crater at all.

"No drive errors," said another. That meant Opportunity had driven in and out without a problem.

Moments later, the hazcam photo confirmed it. The wheel tracks in and out were clear.

Next came the panoramic photos of the rock below: exposed bedrock, with at least six horizontal colored bands running through it.

Could that be sandstone? Laid down by water? Steve wondered. "It feels like the mission has started all over," he marveled.

This false-color image shows visible mineral changes between the materials that make up the rim of Endurance. The cyan blue denotes basalts; the dark green denotes a mixture of iron oxide and basaltic materials; and the reds and yellows indicate dusty material containing sulfates.

Find the RAT holes Opportunity made as he rolled about 39 feet (12 m) into Endurance Crater. How many do you see? Most viewers find it far easier to see the seven holes in an exaggerated color image; the same is true for scientists who are studying the holes from millions of miles away.

The silence was unnerving.

Pink Pools

Exploring deep inside Endurance Crater, Opportunity discovered something odd. Rocks near the top of the crater were full of salt. Deeper down, the rocks had less salt but some amazing crystals. Over a long time, water *can* dissolve salt from rock and form crystals, the scientists knew. It seemed possible, then, that water had once pooled deep in this area. Was the water around long enough for life to form on Mars?

Team members developed a picture of what the area around Endurance might have looked like long ago. Imagine a huge expanse of light tan sand dunes, with ruby red pools under a pink sky. Underground water, stained ruby red from iron, could have risen to the surface and pooled in between the dunes. But the water didn't last long. When it evaporated, the water probably left behind salt grains that blew in the wind, coating everything with red dust.

Scientists believe the pointy features along the snakelike crack in Endurance Crater may have formed when fluids migrated through fractures, depositing minerals. Fracture-filling minerals would have formed veins of a harder material that eroded more slowly than the rock slabs.

As Opportunity crept farther into Endurance Crater, the dune field on the crater floor appeared even more dramatic. This false-color image shows that the dune crests have more dust than the flanks or the flat surfaces between dunes. The blue tint on the flat surfaces results from hematite-containing blueberries. Scientists decided against sending Opportunity to the floor of the crater because it looked like a dangerous sand trap.

6 Can Spirit Climb Up?

Meanwhile, as Opportunity was making discoveries in Endurance Crater, Spirit continued poking around the base of the Columbia Hills. At a planning meeting, team member Justin Maki interrupted. "Hey, a picture of a pretty interesting-looking rock just came down."

This close-up shows the rocky, steep slope up to West Spur, the front hill that Spirit had to get up before she could climb Husband Hill.

"Okay, put it up," said the day's team leader. As the scientists viewed the photos, the room filled with murmurs. This rock was weird, with lots of strange lumps sticking out in all directions.

Larry Soderblom, one of the team leaders, popped his head into the room and gaped at the shape onscreen. "I'm thinking you're probably going to want to get some more pictures of that thing," he said. "That could be the end of the rainbow."

They dubbed the rock Pot of Gold, and sent Spirit in for a closer look. The rock looked like a cross between a potato and an octopus with jellybeans stuck at the end of its tentacles.

The team wanted to RAT it. Spirit thrashed around in the dust and rubble for days trying to get into position. With its bizarre shape, Pot of Gold was a tough RAT target, plus it was barely bigger than the RAT itself. The team aimed the RAT and missed. They missed again. Finally they nicked the target and took some measurements.

Steve Squyres discusses photos from Spirit's travels on Mars at a presentation at Cornell University.

The rock was high in sulfur, chlorine, and phosphorus—minerals often left behind when water evaporates. The minerals were present in a higher concentration than the team had ever measured in other soil on Mars and in much higher amounts than on the Gusev plains.

Pot of Gold was the first water-altered rock that Spirit had encountered.

Finally, what Steve and his team had been waiting for all along!

"Still, there's so much here we don't know," Steve pointed out. "Yes, the Columbia Hills really are dramatically different from the plains around them. But what are they made of? How did they form?"

This close-up image of Pot of Gold has nuggets that appear to stand on the end of stalklike features. The surface of the rock is dotted with pits. Spirit's instruments have shown that Pot of Gold contains high concentrations of minerals left behind when water evaporates.

Sucked into Science

About half the people who had worked on the Mars rover mission were engineers, responsible for operating the robots. "When I started this mission," said Scott Maxwell, "it was all about wanting to drive the rovers. I was happy to be advancing science, but what it comes down to is some rocks and dirt on another planet. And what do I really care?"

Then a funny thing happened. Scott started watching the science team, how they could look at images from the rovers and start telling a story about what may have happened on the surface of another planet a million years ago.

"It was pretty cool," Scott said. "The rest of the engineers got hooked, too. Pretty soon we would start getting images back from the rovers, in the middle of the night, and with no scientists around we'd all be saying to each other, 'Wow! Look at that rock! That's a really cool rock!'"

Engineers were amazed when scientists looked at this image of a rock from Mars and immediately knew it was a meteorite, the first one ever found on a planet other than Earth.

For Spirit, it was climb or die.

Spirit used her panoramic camera to take images combined by scientists to make this downward-looking view. With so much dust on Spirit's solar panels, she seems to blend into her surroundings.

"The dust situation for the two rovers is just very different," said Steve Squyres. "For both, dust is continually falling out of the sky and onto their solar panels. But at Opportunity's site there are all these little puffs of wind that constantly clean the vehicle off. We can't get Opportunity dirty. On Spirit the dust just builds up and builds up and builds up."

Steve studies images from Mars.

Steve didn't know if Spirit would have time to answer his questions. The Martian winter was approaching and the rovers were not designed to survive the brutally cold and dark season. No one had thought the rovers would even make it to winter.

The sun sank lower in the horizon. Spirit's solar power faded. The sun would soon dip so low in the sky that the rover would have trouble gathering enough energy to run her heaters. Her hardware would freeze.

Making things worse, dust was relentlessly piling up on Spirit, coating her solar panels until she almost blended in to her surroundings. No one knew how long she would be able to keep going.

"These are solar-powered vehicles; you have to understand how incredibly important sun is to the rovers," Steve said. "If you are watching them and

suffering with them and rooting for them—you really care about them—then how much dust they have on them and how much sun is shining just means everything."

Yearning for a breakthrough before Spirit's energy faded away, scientists studied nearby Husband Hill. Could Spirit climb it? The slope faced west, away from the precious sunlight. The scientists ran some calculations. They realized that if Spirit took the easiest, quickest route up, which was pointed away from the sun, she would run out of power.

Then the team considered another approach. If Spirit drove along a route that would keep her solar panels pointed directly at the low sun, she might collect enough power to make it up the hill. At the top, she might find clues to help the team understand how the Columbia Hills formed and about the role that water had played in their creation.

Steve appointed Larry Soderblom the chief route-finder for the first mountaineering expedition. Larry's job was to find a path that wouldn't be too steep. A route on good, solid rock instead of crumbly stuff that would slide out from under the rover and drag her down with it.

"Another part of it, which no climber I know has ever had to deal with," Steve noted, "is that we needed to stay on a slope that would keep our solar arrays tilted toward the sun." The task seemed impossible. But for Spirit, it was climb or die.

So Steve sent Spirit picking her way up the slope.

Spirit drove, and then took pictures of the terrain ahead. The scientists made a color-coded map that used red for the spots where the slope tilted toward the sun and blue for areas that faced away from the sun. "The map looked like a big blue pond with red lily pads scattered about," said Steve. Like a frog jumping from lily pad to lily pad,

Colors more clearly indicate the slopes of the Columbia Hills, with red areas representing the gentlest slopes and blue, the steepest. The colors helped Spirit's team find the easiest route up West Spur. Which way would you have sent Spirit?

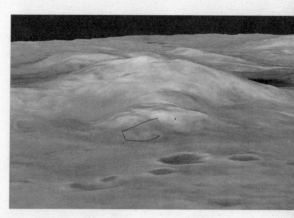

The route Spirit ultimately took up to West Spur.

Spirit traversed the slope. She'd start the day on a red spot, absorbing solar energy. Then she'd scurry across the blue to another red spot, where she'd juice up with more sun.

Spirit crested the ridge.

The rover drivers and the team laughed, slapped one another on the back, and hugged.

"She's a never-give-up, never-say-die rover," Scott Maxwell said proudly. "She climbed a mountain on Mars because that's what it took, dang it!"

"Spirit is such a tough, hard-working, capable vehicle," Steve gushed. "Whatever you give her to do, she just does."

This stunning image is the first 360-degree panorama taken by any rover from the top of a hill on a planet other than Earth. The 470 images of the panorama took a week to send to Earth.

"She's a never-give-up,
never-say-die rover."

7 The Problem with Courage

Opportunity took this photo of his own shadow as he continued into Endurance Crater on sol 180 (July 26, 2004), fully double the rover's primary 90-day mission.

On Opportunity's side of the planet, the sun shone brighter. Little gusts of wind cleaned the dust off his solar panels regularly. And despite his team's worries, Opportunity zipped right out of Endurance Crater.

Nothing seemed to stop this lucky rover. Steve thought back to the first few months of the mission, when Opportunity had finished up his tasks in the landing crater. The team had huddled around an image of the Martian surface, wondering if they could make it to Endurance. "At the far end of the twenty-foot image strip was a monster crater, Victoria," he recalled. "We laughed and said, 'Ah man, what a shame, it would have been cool if we had landed within reach of that thing, ha, ha, ha.'"

In pursuit of speed, the scientists turned off some of the rover's safety features.

But the rover was performing so well and seemed so healthy that Steve steered the team toward an audacious choice. They would send Opportunity toward the biggest challenge yet: Victoria Crater, almost 4 miles (6 km) away. "Victoria was by far the most interesting thing for miles in any direction," said Steve.

Near Endurance, the terrain was very flat and smooth, really easy driving. *Zoom!* Opportunity picked up speed, traveling 100 feet (30 m) a day, 300 feet (90 m) a day, then more than 600 feet (180 m) a day.

As Opportunity headed south, he popped over ripples of sand piled up by the wind. The ripples got bigger and bigger until they were sand dunes. But still the driving seemed effortless. "You'd drive over one, up one side and down the other," Steve said. "We started to get a little cocky." The driving technique his team used, Steve said, could be charitably described as "bombing along at top speed with our eyes closed."

In pursuit of speed, the scientists turned off some of the rover's safety features. One of these, the slip check, let the rover stop and take images to calculate how much he had moved forward and how much his wheels had slipped. "The computer on the rover is very slow, and any time it spends sitting and thinking about what to do next is time it can't spend driving," Steve pointed out. "We told Opportunity to drive, just go. Everything's fine. There's nothing out there."

But that wasn't true.

. . .

It was a stretch to reach Endurance Crater, but Opportunity outlived his 90-day mission and outdrove his 600-meter distance goals to get there. More than a year into his exploration, he headed toward a much more distant goal, Victoria Crater.

On the drive to Victoria Crater, ripples rose up into small dunes. Before taking this picture, Opportunity set a distance record for Martian driving, rolling 582 feet (177.5 m) in a single sol.

"Oh man, this is bad ..."

Opportunity got terribly stuck in Purgatory Dune after he dug himself in up to his hubcaps during the 446th sol of his mission (April 26, 2005). He had completed nearly 131 feet (40 m) of a planned 295-foot (90-m) drive when his wheels began slipping. The wheels kept rotating enough times to have covered the rest of the distance planned for the day if they hadn't been slipping, but the rover barely inched forward. After a turn at the end of the planned drive, Opportunity sensed that he had not turned properly, and stopped moving.

The colors here show relative heights. Red areas are the highest; green areas, the lowest. The difference between red and green is about 28 inches (70 cm). The long dune where Opportunity was stuck is about a foot (1/3 m) tall and 8 feet (2.5 m) wide.

One day, about halfway to Victoria Crater, Opportunity cruised up to the crest of a sand dune. His wheels broke through the thin crust and sank into powdery sand. With the slip check turned off, Opportunity didn't realize he had stopped moving, or that his wheels were slipping, so while his engineers and scientists slept on Earth, he continued to spin his wheels fast. He dug deeper and deeper into the sand.

Steve was back at Cornell University, where his life as a professor of astronomy went on even as the mission continued. That morning, he got himself a cup of Earl Grey tea and turned on his computer to check Opportunity's downlink. Steve was the first to see it: the front and rear cameras clearly showed the two front wheels and two rear wheels buried in silt over their hub caps.

"Oh man, this is bad," Steve muttered.

Opportunity was stuck, really stuck, in a place the team later named Purgatory Dune.

Steve got on the phone to the Jet Propulsion Laboratory in California, three hours behind him. "Hey, guys, we're in trouble here."

The meeting that followed was tense.

"We've got to back out of that sand dune," said rover driver John Wright.

Scott Maxwell agreed.

"Hey, wait a minute," Steve said. "Look, we are in a lot of trouble here. We don't want to do anything that's going to make the situation worse."

So the team stopped Opportunity in his tracks and called back the replica rover for duty. First they made very large quantities of imitation Martian soil. They tinkered with mixtures until they came up with a recipe: equal parts sandbox sand, dry clay, and diatomaceous earth, a powdery substance used in swimming pool filters. Then a bunch of engineers in pickup trucks spanned out across the Los Angeles Basin and hit every Home Depot, buying up literally tons of these ingredients. With wheelbarrows and shovels, and wearing face masks to avoid inhaling the dust, they fashioned the sand and clay, in a giant sandbox, into mounds and pits and dunes, just like on Mars.

Then the team ran the replica rover into the sand until it was stuck. They tried all different ways to wriggle the rover out, rocking it, running its wheels at different speeds, moving its wheels slowly. They wiggled the wheels back and forth to try to make a track out. They tried everything they could imagine.

"It was horrible, really horrible," Steve said. "Not only did we have a rover in trouble, but we had gotten it into trouble. If we had been driving differently it wouldn't have happened, so it was completely our fault. That made it so much harder."

Steve Squyres discovered that Opportunity was stuck in Purgatory Dune while he was working remotely from Cornell University. Here he is pictured at a planning meeting with Professor Jim Bell and students at the Space Sciences building.

It took more than an entire month of experimenting, but the team finally found a strategy they thought would work: they shifted Opportunity into reverse and gunned the engine!

At first they couldn't tell whether Opportunity had moved at all. He spun his wheels backward for weeks. "It was disappointing—discouragingly slow," Steve said. "Our progress in dislodging Opportunity was three to four times slower than our Earth simulation had predicted."

Then, inch by inch, day by day, after six long weeks, Opportunity finally broke free.

"This is so cool!" John said to Scott. The rover drivers were vindicated.

After that ordeal, Opportunity traveled more carefully. He drove a little, took a picture, checked to see if he had moved, checked his tilt and if everything checked out, drove a little farther. Slow and steady, he trekked across the vast Martian plains on his way to Victoria Crater.

"In our wildest dreams we never thought Opportunity would make it all that way," said Steve.

8 A Broken Spirit

Meanwhile, for Spirit, the view from the top of Husband Hill was like standing on the top of the Statue of Liberty. All winter long she snapped pictures, which the scientists strung together into a spectacular 360-degree panorama. "It's one of my favorite images from the entire mission," said Scott Maxwell. "The perspective is amazing—and I know all the hard work it took to get there."

Spirit survived the Martian winter of 2005 and spent another year—that's right, another year!—scouring the treacherous Columbia Hills. "It hit me," Steve said. "Our rovers are the roving geologists I wanted, the geologists who could spot something interesting and go investigate it."

This image of Spirit in the Columbia Hills was produced using Virtual Presence in Space technology, which superimposed an image of a model of Spirit over an actual image from Mars, using Hollywood-style special effects. The size of the rover, estimated on the basis of the size of the rover tracks, is to scale. Images like this one give mission teams a sense of what it would be like if they were there themselves, which helps them plan rover movements.

This false-color view of the outcrop at the top of Husband Hill shows some of the dizzying variety of rocks Spirit discovered in the Columbia Hills.

Rocks looked different in the Columbia Hills, all right. "After the very same old boring basalt for every rock we looked at, there was this bewildering diversity of rocks," said Steve. In fact, there were more than a dozen very distinct types of rocks in these hills.

What had caused all these rocks to be so jumbled together? Rocks began to tell the science team a story, a really exciting story of very early Mars. "It was a violent place, a place bombarded by meteors and ripped apart by volcanic explosions," Steve explained.

"It was a very, very different environment from what we've seen elsewhere on Mars."

Minerals in the rocks indicated that water had been involved. But the team was uncertain of the water's role. They could imagine that steam had hissed up from below, and when it hit hot lava, the lava exploded, scattering rocks in every direction.

"We just couldn't put together a full story of what happened here," said project scientist Joy Crisp. "All we could say for sure was that yes, the rock had been altered by water."

In some ways, how long the rovers have lasted is the biggest mystery, says project scientist Joy Crisp. "Luck," she says. "It's got to be luck." Then she laughs. "It must be those Martian maintenance guys—the AAA on Mars—that are working on them when we're not looking."

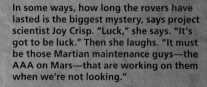

From orbit, this feature looks like the home plate of a baseball diamond, and thus was dubbed Home Plate. Up close it showed the most spectacular layering that Spirit had seen, with a range of grain sizes and textures that changed from the lower to the upper part of the outcrop. Scientists wonder whether Home Plate was formed by volcanoes, impact craters, or water.

This is a virtual simulation of Spirit on Mars as the sun sank below the rim of Gusev Crater. To get the picture of the setting sun, Spirit was commanded to stay awake briefly just before sunset. Because Mars is farther from the sun than the Earth is, the sun appears only about two-thirds the size that it appears to be from Earth.

Weeks and months passed without any other big discoveries. Again and again, Spirit got coated with dust. Over and over, the scientists worried that her power would run out. But it didn't. Despite her dusty solar panels, she kept her batteries charged. Despite the rugged terrain, her systems and her instruments kept on functioning. She outlived everyone's expectations by more than two years.

The Martian winter of 2006 was nearing, but Steve and his team knew what to do. They would send Spirit up nearby McCool Hill, where her panels would face the sun. The rover drivers pointed Spirit in the right direction and along she rolled, dodging rocks, scampering up and down dips in the terrain.

Then Spirit's wheels slipped. She started spinning her wheels without going anywhere. Her wheels sank into the soft sand. Not great news, but the team had been there before. No one panicked.

The team members gathered, some at the Jet Propulsion Laboratory, some remotely. For a few days, the team sent commands and Spirit thrashed around in the sand.

Then one day, the engineer in charge of the rover's mobility expressed alarm. "We've got a problem with the right front wheel," he said. "It seems to have experienced a stall." The team flipped through photos and data, but they couldn't tell what had gone wrong.

"We've had to push Spirit so hard to get anywhere," said Steve. "Something must have broken." Ideas flew around the room. Maybe Spirit was jammed onto a rock and could back her way out. Or maybe a pebble was stuck in the wheel and the team could jiggle it free.

With deep cold and darkness creeping toward their precious rover, all the uncertainty was unsettling.

"Whatever the problem was, we had to diagnose it and deal with it right away," said Steve. "We were not in a good place to spend the winter."

The engineers ran test after test. The right front wheel wouldn't spin. It wouldn't roll. "People were worried," Steve said. "But they were also energized by the challenge. For this team, crisis kicks up the energy level in a way that nothing else does."

Voices became urgent. Discussions intensified. One team member pulled up an image of Spirit's underbelly onscreen. Another brought up a photo of her surroundings. The team created computer animations. They ran the replica rover through its paces. They did everything they could to visualize what it would be like to be Spirit, stuck with a broken wheel in a sandpit on Mars.

"While the intensity level ratcheted up, so did the devotion people felt," Steve said. Everyone was rooting for Spirit, the plucky rover.

"She's a stubborn old girl and she's hanging in there, and she is not going to give up," Scott Maxwell insisted.

Scott was right. The team drove Spirit backward, dragging her bad wheel behind her. Eventually, she lurched free.

But driving wasn't going to be easy. Driving Spirit was like pulling a shopping cart with a dead wheel; she swerved all over the place. It would be slightly easier to pull the bad front wheel rather than push it forward, the team realized, so they decided that the rover would have to spend the rest of her mission driving backward.

And Spirit was still in danger. With a busted wheel, there was no way she could climb McCool Hill. Had she lost her only chance to survive a second Martian winter? The scientists scanned photo after photo, studying the terrain, searching for a low spot where Spirit could face the sun.

They picked Low Ridge, and Spirit limped her way to the top.

There, the little rover was tilted 10 degrees toward the sun. That gave her energy enough to do science for about an hour each day. But not enough power to move.

"We all wanted to get moving again," Steve said.

• • •

"We've had to push Spirit so hard to get anywhere. Something must have broken."

"Look at that!"

The arrival of the Martian spring and summer of 2006 did not bring the victory the team had hoped for. Spirit survived, yes, but she was crippled.

"It was very slow going," Steve lamented. "A measly twenty-meter drive was cause to celebrate. You were ready to pop the champagne when you drove twenty meters with Spirit. It's a really tough vehicle to drive, especially on rugged terrain with all these rocks all around."

The scientists and engineers loved Spirit and her mission, but everything seemed to come more easily to Opportunity. It didn't seem fair.

Then one day, more than three years past her original ninety-day mission, team members noticed something in Spirit's photos.

"Look at that!" Steve gasped. The science team squinted at the photo on the screen.

A strip of soil exposed by Spirit's dragging wheel was bright white, as white as snow.

No one had ever seen soil that color anywhere on Mars.

The team spun Spirit around to investigate. She poked and measured the white soil. It was made of almost pure silica! Such pure silica is

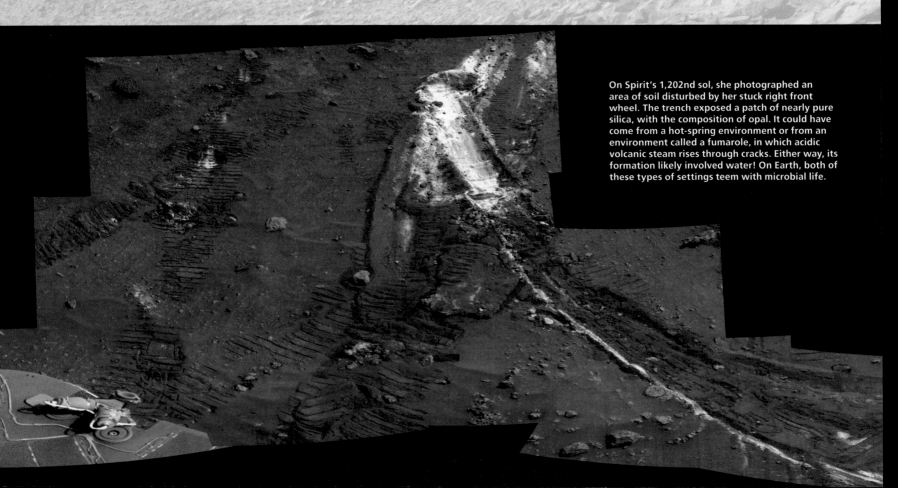

On Spirit's 1,202nd sol, she photographed an area of soil disturbed by her stuck right front wheel. The trench exposed a patch of nearly pure silica, with the composition of opal. It could have come from a hot-spring environment or from an environment called a fumarole, in which acidic volcanic steam rises through cracks. Either way, its formation likely involved water! On Earth, both of these types of settings teem with microbial life.

usually found in only two places on Earth: in hot springs and in volcanic cracks where hot water steams out.

On Earth, both of these places brim with tons of tiny life forms.

This could be it, the team members thought: the most important discovery of Spirit's mission.

Steve and his science team had to know: Was there more silica nearby? If so, did it coat the rocks or was it inside the rocks? They needed to find out whether the hot water was widespread and long-lived. They had to see *inside* nearby rocks.

"We didn't really have anything to break rocks. But we did have the equivalent of a big club in the form of a front wheel that wasn't turning anyway," said Scott Maxwell with a grin. "We decided we might as well use it to smash stuff." So the team aimed Spirit toward a rock and charged at it hoping that she would crush it.

Ready. Set. *Smash*.

Spirit swerved on her broken wheel and missed the target rock.

But she hit a different rock, which the team named Innocent Bystander. The rock cracked wide open.

It was rich with silica.

Now the scientists and engineers knew for certain: this area once had an environment capable of supporting life! Spirit had indeed made the most important discovery of her mission—and the discovery never would have happened if she hadn't busted her wheel.

Spirit's team, who had struggled with her through it all, whooped with joy.

"The fact that we found [this] after nearly twelve hundred days on Mars . . . makes you wonder what else is still out there," said Steve.

Steve Squyres at the world premiere of the IMAX film *Roving Mars* in Washington, D.C.

9 Opportunity's Last Stand?

This image from the High Resolution Imaging Science Experiment on NASA's Mars Reconnaissance Orbiter shows Opportunity near the rim of Victoria Crater, wheel tracks in the soil behind it.

Opportunity's epic journey across the Martian plains lasted for almost two years—and his whole mission was supposed to last only three months. Finally, in late summer 2006, he reached Victoria Crater!

People on Earth were astonished that Opportunity had made it. Headlines across the world proclaimed his achievement: "Crater Whets Curiosity"; "Mars Crater Is a Dream Come True"; "Epic Trek by Mars Rover May Unlock Secrets of Watery Past." Steve and his team couldn't have been more proud.

"For twenty-one months we trudged endlessly across these plains," Steve said. "Then one day we are right at the rim of it—POW! There's just this spectacular scenery, this fabulous geology right in front of us."

"CRATER WHETS CURIOSITY"

"MARS CRATER IS A DREAM COME TRUE"

"EPIC TREK BY MARS ROVER MAY UNLOCK SECRETS OF WATERY PAST"

This image superimposes an artist's concept of Opportunity on the rim of Victoria Crater, to give a sense of scale. "What these rovers have done is that they've made Mars a familiar place," John Callas pointed out. "Mars is now our neighborhood. My team goes to work on Mars every day. Mars is no longer this strange, unknown world."

This image shows how badly the dust storm blocked Opportunity's sun. The numbers across the top of the image report a measurement of atmospheric opacity, called by the Greek letter tau. The higher the number, the darker the sky.

τ = 0.94   2.9   4.1   3.8   4.7

Opportunity Sol Number and Local True Solar Time

Afraid to lose the lucky rover, Steve and his team decided that Opportunity should slowly circle the crater, thoroughly exploring the edges and looking for the safest way in. After a year of observing the rim, the team picked Duck Bay as the entry point. With its slopes of 15 to 20 degrees and exposed bedrock, it offered the best chance of safe driving.

At last, Opportunity's scientists gave him the green light. Standing on the rim, ready to roll into the huge crater, he was about to make his boldest move ever.

Suddenly, *whoosh*, a huge dust storm blew in, so big it blocked out the sun. The storm grew. It smothered the planet with thick red dust. The dust was much worse on Opportunity's side of the planet than on Spirit's.

Without sunlight, Opportunity couldn't recharge his batteries. Dust blew for weeks. The rover's power drained away.

"It blew up on us, just blew up into a massive global dust storm," said Steve. "The entire surface of the planet was just completely invisible from space. The sky grew so dark." It got so bad that the scientists tried to have the rover take pictures of the sun, but they couldn't even find it.

"We hadn't seen anything of that magnitude before," said mission manager Colette Lohr. "It was very stressful."

Suddenly, a tiny flaw, one the team had known about since the rover landed, became a big problem. Opportunity's arm has joints—like a shoulder, elbow, and wrist. Each joint has a heater that warms it up when the scientists want to use the arm. Since the day Opportunity landed, the heater on his shoulder joint had been stuck on. This little heater used up precious energy. And in the dust storm, Opportunity could not afford to lose any energy.

Battery power drained. Temperatures fell. "This is really looking bad," Steve said. "It's really, really scary."

In computer code, the team sent Opportunity the equivalent of this message: "Don't talk to us. Don't try to do anything. Three days from now, send us a tiny little beep, a tiny burst of data to let us know how you are doing. Then sleep some more."

"I had this horrible, helpless feeling because there was nothing we could do," Steve said. "It was like Mars was trying to kill our machine."

For days, team members sat at their computers, waiting for a sign. "It was touch and go," said John Callas, the lead engineer at the time. "We didn't know when we came in the next day if the rover would still be there."

The scientists walked around in a daze. Opportunity had driven twenty-one months—nearly two years—to reach Victoria Crater, then spent almost another year along the rim. And here, at the edge of new discoveries, the mission might end.

Without the sun's warming rays, Mars grew even colder. No one knew how much longer the little rover could last. If the storm went on, Opportunity might not have enough power to wake up. Weeks went by, and the power dwindled. "I think we're going to lose Opportunity," said Steve.

Dust fell from the sky, thickening the coat on Opportunity's solar panels. The team watched and waited and worried.

• • •

"It blew up on us, just blew up into a massive global dust storm."

"I think we're going to lose Opportunity."

Steve worries about his rovers from afar, at his office at Cornell University.

Wet Mars

More of the same. That's what Steve and his team found in Victoria Crater. This may sound boring to some, but to the geologists, it was exciting. That's because they know it could mean the difference between discovering an ancient puddle on Mars and an ancient ocean! When Opportunity crawled 30 feet (9 m) deep into Victoria, he found the same blueberry-shaped rocks that he had found in Eagle and Endurance Craters. This suggested that when water was present on Mars, it was widespread, not confined to one spot. And the deeper Opportunity probed, the bigger the blueberries he found, suggesting that water had repeatedly come and gone billions of years ago.

Then, little by little, the sky cleared.

Opportunity sent a message: he was alive! Mission Control erupted into cheers.

A gust of wind cleared the dust from the rover's solar panels. Opportunity peered over the crater rim. Then he rolled down, down into Victoria Crater, bringing the team once again to a place they'd never been before.

Opportunity explored the great Victoria Crater for a year. In the fall of 2008, when the scientists had learned all they could there, Steve asked his team, "What is the most different thing—something

we haven't seen on Mars—that is as important as anything we can imagine in Mars science?"

The answer was Endeavor Crater. Images from the *Mars Express* orbiter showed that the rim of the 14-mile-wide crater was rich with phyllosilicates, or clay. The rovers had never studied clay. And clay was intriguing because it generally forms in relatively neutral water. That's important, because life is more likely to survive in neutral water than in water that's acidic.

Does Opportunity have any chance of getting there? the team asked. The huge crater was 7 miles (12 km) away, as far as the rover had already

Opportunity sent a message: he was alive!

traveled since landing on Mars. Even at a quick pace of 110 yards a day, the trip could take two years.

"It's a long shot," Steve admitted.

But what in this mission *hadn't* been a long shot?

"It's funny. When we first built [the rovers], we babied them, we coddled them, we dressed up in funny suits, we had rubber gloves on, we tiptoed around them and were extremely careful," said Steve. "Now they are scratched, beat up, and dirty. We have pushed them to their limits on Mars, climbing the steepest slopes that they could climb, going down slippery inclines, and drilling RAT holes into rocks while perched on a precarious slope." But Steve, his team, and his rover were ready for another adventure. With Steve's blessing, Opportunity rolled on.

On May 20, 2010, Opportunity broke the record for the longest mission operating on another planet's surface. The record set by the *Viking 1 Lander* was 6 years and 116 days. Each day that Opportunity continues to explore, he sets another record.

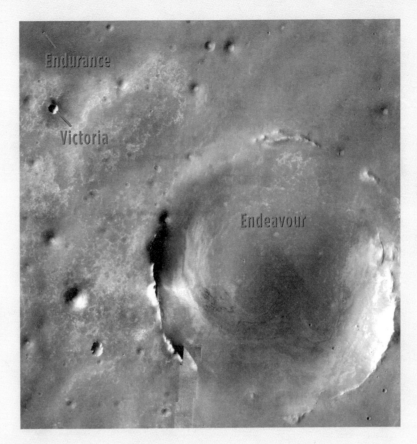

During Opportunity's amazingly long mission, he visited ever-grander craters. Opportunity exited Victoria Crater on August 28, 2008, after nearly a year investigating the interior. Here he was on his way to the biggest one ever: Endeavor. It is about 13.7 miles (22 km) in diameter and about 1,000 feet (300 m) deep. The rover had already operated more than eighteen times longer than originally planned, and the distance to Endeavor, about 7 miles (12 km), matched the total distance Opportunity had driven since landing in early 2004.

During the fourth anniversary of his landing on Mars, Opportunity examined rocks inside the alcove Duck Bay, especially the band exposed around the interior of Victoria Crater, about 20 feet (6 m) from the rim.

10 Free Spirit

In the spring of 2009, as Spirit continued her exploration of the Columbia Hills, her wheels fell through some crust. Hiding underneath: slippery sand.

Steve wasn't immediately alarmed. Things like this had happened before.

Spirit, it seemed, was straddling the edge of a 26-foot-wide crater in a region called Troy. The team commanded her to continue driving backward, hoping she would plow through the problem. But her left side sank deeper into the nasty, loose, fluffy sand. Spirit spun her wheels. She just couldn't get a grip.

Spirit slipped in soft ground during short backward drives on the 1,886th and 1,889th sols of her mission on Mars (April 23 and 26, 2009). This view is looking northward, with Husband Hill on the horizon. Spirit used her front hazard-avoidance camera after driving on sol 1,889 to get this wide-angle view, which shows the soil that was disturbed by the drives.

Rover team members Kim Lichtenberg (left) and Mike Seibert fill a mixer with powdered clay and diatomaceous earth, a combination thought to simulate the soil where Spirit is stuck on Mars.

The rover had come from more solid terrain, so the team decided to retrace her steps. Still, she made no progress.

Then another wheel stalled. While investigating the reason, the scientists discovered a pile of rocks under the rover. If she got lodged onto the rocks, she could be stuck there forever.

Lead engineer John Callas suggested a stand-down. Steve agreed. They wouldn't move Spirit again until they tested their options on the replica rover on Earth.

In a huge sandbox filled with a pale yellow powder, engineers placed the replica rover tilting toward the left with its three downhill wheels buried. The make-believe Mars dust was soft, fluffy, and fine. Squeezing it hardly compacted it. Instead, the soft sand squirted out like water. Weight placed on its surface sank with little resistance.

The team tried driving the replica straight ahead and straight backward. They tested going back in a sharp arc uphill. They spun its wheels in place, pointing uphill, and spun them in the other direction, pointing downhill. They wiggled the wheels driving forward and backward. They spun the wheels forward on one side and backward on the other.

For seven months, nothing worked better than anything else. The replica rover barely moved.

"The only way to learn anything more was to try it on Mars," Steve said. So the team put Spirit through her paces. They tried to . . .

Drive forward spinning the wheels at different speeds. No good.

Drive forward steering the wheels back and forth. No progress.

Drive forward with the wheels turned sharply. Nothing.

The campaign to "Free Spirit" went global with T-shirts and bumper stickers. Hundreds of people e-mailed NASA with suggestions. But nothing worked.

After exhausting all the options driving forward, the team tried driving backward again.

In ten drives, Spirit moved about a foot (34 cm), far more than she had moved driving forward.

"Emotionally it's been harder than I thought it would be. It's just uncomfortable not to be hearing from our rover."

Rover team members Mike Seibert (left) and Paolo Bellutta add a barrowful of soil mixture to the sloped box where a test rover will be used to conduct maneuvers that might help the team wriggle Spirit free from her sand trap on Mars.

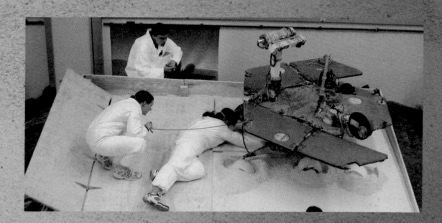

Engineers placed a rock underneath the test rover to closely simulate Spirit's predicament on Mars. After becoming embedded in soft soil, Spirit used the microscopic imager at the end of her arm to look under her own belly, confirming that a rock that lay beneath her was touching her underbelly.

Rover team members check slight movements by the test rover. From left: Alfonso Herrera, Matt Van Kirk, Mike Seibert, and Brenda Franklin.

pride. When the rovers are doing well, you're proud of them, and when they do badly, you're angry. And if they're about to stop doing what they do best, that's sad."

On February 8, 2010, without enough power to drive the rover, the team ceased its efforts. Spirit would stay where she was for the long Martian winter.

Two months later, on March 30, 2010, Spirit didn't communicate with the team at the appointed time. As expected, she had gone into "low-power fault," shutting down all systems not required to survive, including communications. "I'll be honest," said Steve. "It hit me harder than I thought it would. I've been saying it was going to happen; we all knew it was going to happen. It's the right thing. It's what the rover is supposed to do. But emotionally it's been harder than I thought it would be. It's just uncomfortable not to be hearing from our rover. We are not going to hear from her possibly for months, and that's really hard."

Steve hopes the sun will charge Spirit's batteries enough so she can phone home. "I still think we are going to hear from Spirit again," Steve said, "and that we've got lots of exploring ahead of us."

But if Spirit shuts down the mission clock to save power, she may not know when to send a signal. Then it could be a full Earth year before the Martian summer sun blasts the solar arrays enough to fully wake up the rover.

Filled with hope, the team worked feverishly. But Martian winter was setting in for the fourth time since the rover's arrival on the planet. Spirit was tilted away from the sun, which hung lower in the horizon. She struggled to absorb enough energy to drive.

This logo was designed for the campaign to free Spirit from where she became trapped in a sandpit in an area called Troy.

The team was forced to drive the rover less and less frequently. Spirit had to spend days at a time recharging just to gain enough power to move.

Spirit's last chance to move before power dropped too low came quickly. Team members gathered for their final plan. "We're scientists and engineers, but we're human, too," Steve said. "Over the course of a mission like this you get very attached to these things. You attach so many hopes, dreams, frustrations,

"I'm going to be the last guy to turn off the lights on this mission."

Steve Squyres at a press briefing in Washington, D.C.

What if the team doesn't hear from Spirit then?

"It could be that Spirit is covered in dust and we have to wait for a gust to clear her solar panels," said Steve hopefully.

Steve and the team are prepared to wait. "There is a saying among the team members," said rover driver Ashley Stroupe, "that you don't bet against Spirit."

"I've begun to think of Spirit as being the Indiana Jones of Mars," said team member Scott Maxwell. "These impossible challenges just get dumped on her, but somehow she manages to roll under that closing door, and go back for her hat and keep on going."

"The bottom line is we're not giving up on Spirit," said Steve. "We're going to keep listening."

Then Steve took a deep breath. His voice softened. "I'm going to be the last guy to turn off the lights on this mission," he said.

11 Mission More Than Accomplished!

Steve and his team of scientists and engineers expected the rovers to last three months, tops. Spirit and Opportunity endured for more than six *years*—and scientists are still counting. These little machines explored a record-breaking 25 miles (44 km) of Mars's surface and snapped more than a quarter of a million photos there, including 360-degree views of hills, plains, and craters. They became so much more than rovers. They did the work of geologists, meteorologists, chemists, photographers, mountain climbers, and crater trekkers.

The rovers survived three Martian winters and a sun-blocking dust storm. They have been more successful than anyone dreamed. Spirit explored high into the Columbia Hills, scaling a 30-degree incline and reaching the 269-foot (82-m) summit of Husband Hill, the highest peak in the range. Opportunity explored deep into Eagle, Endurance, and Victoria Craters. Together, the two rovers covered more of the surface of Mars than any other mission.

"What connects all this for me is that I simply love to explore," Steve said. "I love doing something nobody else has done, going someplace no one has ever been, discovering stuff no one has ever seen."

Spirit and Opportunity have changed the way we look at the red planet. Because of the photos they sent us daily over the course of six years, Mars has become a familiar place: less alien— more like our neighbor, more like our own planet.

Most important, the rovers have answered important scientific questions: Was there water on Mars? Yes. Was it deep and warm and lasting? Yes again! Thanks to Spirit and Opportunity, the possibility that life once existed on Mars seems stronger than ever. If life once thrived on our neighboring planet, maybe someday we'll find it on other planets, too.

But there is still more to learn about Mars. "The more we know about the weather, the wind, and the dust on the red planet," Steve said, "the better scientists and engineers can succeed with the ultimate dream: putting people on Mars." He thinks it can happen in just ten or fifteen years.

"The rovers are our surrogates, our robotic precursors to a world that, as humans, we're still not quite ready to visit," Steve said. "And that's what I really want to see change. There are many things I could wish for our rovers, but in the end, there's only one that matters. What I really want, more than anything else, is boot prints in our wheel tracks."

Maybe they will be yours.

Tracks showing where Opportunity rolled in and out of Victoria Crater.

Steve Squyres and colleague Mark Boyles celebrate Thursday, January 15, 2004, at NASA's Jet Propulsion Laboratory, in Pasadena, California, after receiving confirmation that Spirit rolled off her lander and onto the surface of Mars. "That was one of the happiest moments of my life," Steve says.

Curiosity Continues

In August 2012, if all goes well, another rover will set down on Mars, this time lowered to the planet's surface from a sky crane. The Mars Science Laboratory, named Curiosity, is a supersized rover, with a long neck and one wide pink eye that can vaporize rocks. Nine feet long (2.7 m), 1,875 pounds (850 kg), made mostly of aluminum, and powered by a nuclear generator, Curiosity will search Mars for organic molecules, the chemical building blocks of life.

The car-size Curiosity is about twice as long and more than five times as heavy as Spirit and Opportunity. It will be hard to match Spirit and Opportunity's toughness, but Curiosity is designed to have a greater range, more instruments, and a bigger, stronger robotic arm. "It's being built by the same team of people, so there's a great deal in common, just scaled up," Steve pointed out. "The six-wheel suspension system, the camera mast, the arm on the front—it's conceptually very similar. We retained everything that worked well and then built on it."

Steve is again part of the team, working on three of the instruments that will head to Mars on Curiosity. One, called APXS, was copied straight from the twin rovers. It will be able to determine the amounts of major elements in samples, but faster than before. Instead of hours, it can get a measurement in minutes.

Steve is also collaborating on a newer instrument called DAN. Tucked under the rover, DAN will be able to measure the average load of hydrogen in the ground below. Lots of hydrogen may suggest an environment favorable for life.

The crowning achievement will be Curiosity's onboard lab. SAM, short for Sample Analysis at Mars, can sniff the air searching for chemicals such as methane, which can be released by microbes. When SAM sniffs something promising, vents will open so it can take samples from the air and study them. SAM will also bake rock and soil samples in its oven and then sniff and study the gases that are released. And it will be able to detect organic compounds, the building blocks of life.

What better way to search for life on Mars than to search directly for evidence of life on Mars? Steve asked. And what could be better than sending a rolling geologist to Mars? Sending one that brings along its own lab!

What better way to search for life on Mars than to search directly for evidence of life?

This is an artist conception of Curiosity on Mars. Curiosity is slated to land in Gale Crater (far left), a 96-mile-wide (154-km) crater at the base of a mountain taller than Mount Rainier. Curiosity will explore this dramatic terrain for one martian year —almost two Earth years. And maybe longer . . .

For an amazing animation of Curiosity's landing and the work it will do on the red planet, visit www.nasa.gov/mission_pages/msl/index.html.

Mission Update

On May 25, 2011, after 1,200 attempts to contact Spirit, NASA announced it would no longer send daily wake-up calls to the stuck rover. The extreme cold of the Martian winter likely damaged Spirit's electronics. "It's very sad to lose Spirit," Steve said. "But she accomplished so much more than any of us expected; the sadness is very much tempered with satisfaction and pride."

After a journey of almost *three years*, Opportunity defied all odds, beat all expectations, and reached Endeavor Crater on August 9, 2011! When this book went to press, Opportunity had traveled more than 20 miles (34 km), more than *fifty* times the distance originally planned for the mission. To find out what the amazing rover has discovered in the clays of the 14-mile-wide (22 km) crater, check NASA's mission website at www.marsrover.nasa.gov or visit the author's website at www.elizabethrusch.com.

Sources

Callas, John. Project manager of the Mars Exploration Rovers since 2006. In-person interview with the author, February 2010.

Chang, Kenneth. "Rover Heads to New Crater." *New York Times*, September 23, 2008.

Crisp, Joy. Deputy project scientist for the Mars Science Laboratory since 2006; project scientist for the Mars Exploration Rovers 2000–2006. In-person interview with author, February 2010.

Darling, David. *The Complete Book of Spaceflight: From Apollo 1 to Zero Gravity*. Hoboken, N.J.: John Wiley & Sons, 2003.

Fountain, Henry. "Crater Was Shaped by Wind and Water Mars Rover Data Shows." *New York Times*, May 26, 2009.

Golombek, Matt. Mars Exploration Landing Site scientist since 2000, Mars Exploration Rover Science Operations Working Group chair, Long-Term Planning Science Group lead, and Geology Science Group lead since 2002. In-person interview with author, February 2010.

Kaufman, Mark. "Mars Crater Is a Dream Come True." *Washington Post*, September 28, 2006.

Maxwell, Scott. Mars Exploration rover driver. In-person interview with author, February 2010.

Moshowitz, Clara. "Trapped Mars Rovers Turning New Corner, Scientists Say." *Space.com*, January 27, 2010.

NASA/JPL archive. "Mission Fantastic to Mars." *Spotlight on Mars*, 2004, marsrover.nasa.gov/spotlight/20040810.html.

———. "Machinists to the Stars." *Spotlight on Mars*, 2001, marsrover.nasa.gov/spotlight/machinists01.html.

———. "What's in a Name? It Depends on Who's Doing the Naming." *Spotlight on Mars*, June 2, 2004.

NASA/JPL Press Release No. 2003-081. *Girl with Dreams Names Mars Rovers "Spirit" and "Opportunity."* June 8, 2003.

NASA/JPL Press Release No. 2010-030. "Now a Stationary Research Platform, NASA's Mars Rover Spirit Starts a New Chapter in Red Planet Scientific Studies." January 26, 2010.

NASA/JPL Video. *Three Years on Mars: Spirit's Story*. January 4, 2007.

———. *Entering Endurance Crater*. June 21, 2004.

———. *Spirit: Six Years of Roving Mars*. January 26, 2010.

———. *Five Years on Mars*. December 22, 2008.

———. *Five Years and Still Roving on Mars: Opportunity*. January 15, 2009.

Perlman, David. "NASA Gives Up Effort to Free Mars Rover." *San Francisco Chronicle*, January 27, 2010.

Smith, Lewis. "Epic Trek by Mars Rover May Unlock Secrets of Water Past." *Times* (UK), October 3, 2006.

Squyres, Steve. Principal investigator for the Mars Exploration Rover mission. Recorded telephone interviews with author, December 17, 2007; February 8, 2010; February 15, 2010; March 8, 2010; March 31, 2010.

———. *Roving Mars: Spirit, Opportunity, and the Exploration of the Red Planet*. New York: Hyperion, 2005. Quotes reprinted with permission from Hyperion.

"Crater Whets Curiosity." *Sunday Herald Sun* (Melbourne), October 8, 2006.

Tyell, David. "An Ancient Martian Volcanic Blast." *Sky and Telescope*, August 2007, p. 17.

Wright, John. Rover driver's blog.

JPL's Mars Exploration Rovers Mission website: marsrover.nasa.gov/home.

Chapter Notes

1. Mission Impossible

"I loved watching . . .": Squyres, interview.
"But after studying . . .": Squyres, interview.
"Suddenly, I was talking . . .": Squyres, interview.
"Instead, I was in that room . . .": Squyres, *Roving Mars*.
"But even more obvious . . .": Squyres, interview.
"Imagine you're a geologist . . .": Squyres, interview.
"I walked out of that room . . .": Squyres, *Roving Mars*.
"Just once I wanted . . .": Squyres, interview.
"You start off with nothing . . .": Squyres, *Roving Mars*.
"I imagined . . .": Squyres, interview.
"Rovers are risky . . .": Squyres, interview.
"I'm stubborn . . .": Squyres, interview.

2. The Making of the Mars Rovers

"Can you build two? . . .": Squyres, *Roving Mars*.
"Our schedule . . .": Squyres, *Roving Mars*.
"I love the process . . .": Squyres, interview.
"After all the years of hope . . .": Squyres, *Roving Mars*.

"Sun is so important...": Squyres, interview.

"I do my best...": Squyres, *Roving Mars*.

"We had done our best...": Squyres, *Roving Mars*.

"I'm embarrassed to admit...": Squyres, *Roving Mars*.

"I used to live...": NASA/JPL Press Release No. 2003-081.

3. Are We Really on Mars?

"We would be helpless...": Squyres, interview.

"I tore mine open...": Squyres, *Roving Mars*.

"We have a signal...It works, man...": Quotes only, Squyres, *Roving Mars*.

"We haven't heard anything...It hit me then...": Quotes only, Squyres, *Roving Mars*.

"Holy smokes...This is the sweetest...": Quotes only, Squyres, *Roving Mars*.

"They were the strangest...": Squyres, interview.

"We treated the rovers...": Maxwell, interview.

"Evidence pointed...": Squyres, interview.

"Part of the game...": Maxwell, interview.

"You get a beep...": Golombek, interview.

"We landed and *boom*...": Squyres, interview.

"OK, you're in charge...": NASA/JPL archive, "What's in a Name?"

"Whenever explorers go...": NASA/JPL archive, "What's in a Name?"

4. Hitting the Dusty Trail

"Okay, so what...The Spirit was willing...": Quotes only, Squyres, *Roving Mars*.

"We hit it with...": Squyres, interview.

"How about the Columbia...": Squyres, interview.

"But the hills are the only...": Squyres, interview.

"There's a very good chance...": Squyres, *Roving Mars*.

"It's clearly outside...": Squyres, interview.

"We just pushed the pedal...": Squyres, interview.

"Spirit's site...": Squyres, interview.

5. Can Opportunity Climb Down?

"The whole thing...": Squyres, *Roving Mars*.

"I couldn't wait...": Squyres, interview.

"So here's the problem...": Squyres, *Roving Mars*.

"That's ten times more...": Squyres, interview.

"I would plan...": NASA/JPL Video. *Entering Endurance Crater*.

"If we can't climb...": NASA/JPL Video. *Entering Endurance Crater*.

"Opportunity has to die...": Squyres, *Roving Mars*.

"We can't use that...And the thing...": Quotes only, Squyres, *Roving Mars*.

"We'll work our way...": Squyres, *Roving Mars*.

"Tilt is nine...It feels like...": Quotes only, Squyres, *Roving Mars*.

6. Can Spirit Climb Up?

"Hey, a picture of...I'm thinking...": Squyres, *Roving Mars*.

"Still, there's so much here...": Squyres, interview.

"These are solar-powered vehicles...": Squyres, interview.

"Another part of it...": Squyres, *Roving Mars*.

"The map looked like...": Squyres, interview.

"She's a never-give-up...": Maxwell, interview.

"Spirit is such a...": Squyres, interview.

"When the mission started...": Maxwell, interview.

"It was pretty cool...": Maxwell, interview.

"Wow, look at that...": Maxwell, interview.

7. The Problem with Courage

"At the far end...": Squyres, interview.

"Victoria was by far...": Squyres, interview.

"You'd drive over one...": Squyres, interview.

"The computer on the rover...": Squyres, interview.

"We told Opportunity to drive...": Squyres, interview.

"Oh man, this is bad...Hey, guys...": Squyres, interview.

"We've got to back...": John Wright's blog.

"Hey, wait...": Squyres, interview.

"It was horrible...": Squyres, interview.

"It was disappointing...": Squyres, interview.

"This is so cool!...": John Wright's blog.

"In our wildest dreams...": Squyres, interview.

8. A Broken Spirit

"It's one of my favorite...": Maxwell, interview.

"It hit me...": Squyres, interview.

"After all the very same...": Squyres, interview.

"It was a violent place...": Squyres, interview.

"We just couldn't...": Crisp, interview.

"We've got a problem...": Squyres, interview.

"We've had to push...": Squyres, interview.

"Whatever the problem was...": Squyres, interview.

"People were worried...": Squyres, interview.

"While the intensity...": Squyres, interview.

"She's a stubborn old girl...": NASA/JPL Video. *Three Years on Mars: Spirit's Story*.

"We all wanted...": Squyres, interview.

"It was very slow going...": Squyres, interview.

"Look at that...": Squyres, interview.

"We didn't really have...": Maxwell, interview.

"The fact that we found...": Tyell, article.

9. Opportunity's Last Stand?

"'Crater Whets'...": *Sunday Herald Sun*.

"'Mars Crater Is'...": Kaufman, article.

"'Epic Trek'...": Smith, article.

"For twenty-one months...": NASA/JPL Video. *Five Years on Mars*.

"It blew up on us...": Squyres, interview.

"We hadn't seen anything...": NASA/JPL Video. *Five Years and Still Roving on Mars: Opportunity*.

"This is really looking...": Squyres, interview.

"Don't talk to us...": Squyres, interview.

"I had this horrible...": Squyres, interview.

"It was touch and go...": NASA/JPL Video. *Five Years and Still Roving on Mars: Opportunity*.

"I think we're going to lose...": Squyres, interview.

"What is the most different thing...": Golombek, interview.

"It's a long shot...": Chang, article.

"It's funny...": NASA/JPL archive. "Mission Fantastic to Mars."

10. Free Spirit

"The only way to learn...": Squyres, interview.

"We're scientists...": Moshowitz, article.

"I'll be honest...": Squyres, interview.

"I still think...": Squyres, interview.

"It could be...": Squyres, interview.

"There is a saying...": NASA/JPL Video. *Spirit: Six Years of Roving Mars*.

"I've begun to think...": NASA/JPL Video. *Spirit: Six Years of Roving Mars*.

"The bottom line...": Squyres, interview.

"I'm going to be the last guy...": Squyres, interview.

"[This is] so different...": Perlman, article.

11. Mission More Than Accomplished!

"What connects all this...": Squyres, interview.

"The more we know...": Squyres, interview.

"The rovers are our surrogates...": Squyres, *Roving Mars*.

"It's being built by the same...": Squyres, interview.

For Further Exploration

The author has been reading newspaper, magazine, and web articles and NASA/JPL mission updates and press releases and viewing photos and videos on the Mars rovers for more than six years. These sources number in the thousands, and it would be impossible to list them all here. Below are some excellent and entertaining resources readers might like to explore.

Grab your 3D glasses and see what the red planet really looks like

Jim Bell, *Mars 3-D: A Rover's-Eye View of the Red Planet* (New York: Sterling, 2008).

Spirit 3-D images: marsrovers.jpl.nasa.gov/gallery/3d/spirit.

Opportunity 3-D images: marsrovers.jpl.nasa.gov/gallery/3d/opportunity.

Multimedia

George Butler, *Roving Mars* (Walt Disney Pictures, 2007).

Sid Lieberman, *Twelve Years on Mars*. An audio recording of the storyteller commissioned by NASA and Jet Propulsion Laboratory to tell the story of the Mars rover landing. Download it for free at http://www.sydlieberman.com/recordings/index.php.

Scott Maxwell, *Mars and Me: The Unofficial Diary of a Mars Rover Driver, Five Years Delayed Blog*: marsandme.blogspot.com.
NASA/JPL's multimedia section, where you can view dozens of videos of the Mars rover mission, including interviews with scientists and engineers and thousands of photos: marsrover.nasa.gov/gallery.

Websites

JPL's Mars Exploration Rover website: marsrover.nasa.gov. You'll find it all here—mission updates, articles, photos, videos, hands-on activities, contests, and press releases. It's the most complete site on the mission.

Athena Mars Exploration Rover website: athena.cornell.edu. Cornell University's site on the Mars rovers, with great information on the rovers' science tools and the early days of the mission.

NASA's Solar System Exploration website: solarsystem.nasa.gov/planets/profile.cfm?Object=Mars. Excellent background information on Mars and all the other planets and objects in our solar system.

Also at solarsystem.nasa.gov/missions/profile.cfm, you can learn about all Mars missions, past, present and future. Type "Mars" in for the target.

Images from the High Resolution Imaging Science Experiment, as well as further information about the Mars Reconnaissance Orbiter, are available online at www.nasa.gov/mro or http://HiRISE.lpl.arizona.edu.

Archives

Mission updates: More than six years of daily or weekly updates on each rover can be found at marsrover.nasa.gov/mission/status_spirit.html and at marsrover.nasa.gov/mission/status_opportunity.html.

Mission photos: All the photos from this mission—and from other Mars missions—are available to view and download at the NASA/JPL Photojournal site photojournal.jpl.nasa.gov/targetFamily/Mars.

Acknowledgments

Steve Squyres, creator of Spirit and Opportunity, says he loves the little rovers. And they were built by a loving family. I want to join Steve in thanking the more than four thousand people who made this mission possible, from the scientists and engineers who designed, built, tested, flew, and managed the rovers, to the seamstresses who sewed the parachutes and the webmasters who uploaded the photos onto the Internet.

It takes a loving family to make a book like this possible as well. I would like to thank my husband, Craig, who first followed the rovers' adventures and urged me to write a children's book about them. My deep appreciation goes to Melissa Dalton and Michelle Blair for their stellar research, editing, and transcribing skills and to Addie Boswell, Nancy Coffelt, Ruth Feldman, Kim Griswell, Barbara Kerley, Amber Keyser, Michelle McCann, Sabina Rascol, Mary Rehmann, Izzi Rusch, Cobi Rusch, Nicole Schrieber, and the students of Chapman Elementary School in Portland, Oregon, for their insightful comments. Special thanks to JPL's Guy Webster for arranging my visit to JPL and for hosting me there and answering countless questions. Thanks to my editors Erica Zappy, Ann Rider, and Christine Krones and their team at Houghton Mifflin for feeding my passion for this story and for developing their own passion for the precious Mars rovers.

Finally, I want to thank Steve Squyres. He has worked for more than a decade to make his dream of rovers on Mars come true. Steve told me he had two goals for the mission. Most people know the first one: to learn more about Mars. But he also wanted the rovers to rekindle a public passion for exploration, especially among young people. "I've been thinking about the legacy of this mission," he told me. "Exciting young people may actually be more important than anything we learn about sulfates on Mars."

In the midst of leading the complex mission, teaching future astronomers at Cornell University, and making time for his family, Steve paused many times to tell me the riveting story of the Mars rovers. Steve, thank you for your generosity, your passion, and for your deep commitment to educating and inspiring young people.

Photo Credits

All photos are courtesy of NASA/JPL except:
Pages 6, 11 (top right), 20, 22, 23 30 (large): NASA
8 (all), 10 (bottom two): Squyres family
9: Neil Armstrong, NASA
10 (top left), 12, 16 (middle both and bottom), 18 (both), 19 (both), 21, 29 (bottom right), 31 (bottom right), 34–35 (bottom), 36 (left), 37 (middle), 38 (bottom), 42, 52 (both), 54 (both), 57 (middle right), 68 (bottom left), 69 (both): NASA/JPL
11, 33 (left): NASA/JPL/USGS
13 (bottom), 41 (top), 47 (top middle), 49 (left), 55, 61, 65, 71: Cornell University Photography
15: David McNew/Getty Images

Glossary

APXS: alpha particle x-ray spectrometer. An instrument on the rover's arm that measures concentrations of chemical elements.

ATLO: Assembly, Test, and Launch Operations. The process of building, testing, and launching a spacecraft.

Basalt: A common form of volcanic rock.

Bedrock: Solid rock found under dust, soil, or loose rocks.

Crater: A bowl-shaped hole made by a meteorite, explosion, or volcanic activity.

Delta 2: A rocket built by Boeing that was used to launch Spirit and Opportunity.

DSN: Deep Space Network. A network of satellite dishes in Gladstone, California, near Madrid, Spain; and in Tidbinbilla, Australia, that NASA uses to communicate with spacecraft beyond Earth's orbit.

Dust devil: A mini tornado that blows across the surface of a planet.

EDL: Entry, Descent, and Landing. The process of entering a planet's atmosphere and landing on its surface.

Hazcam: Hazard avoidance camera. Hazcams were located in the front and back of the Mars rovers to help avoid obstacles while driving.

Hematite: An iron mineral that usually requires water to form.

In Situ Instruments Laboratory: The room at JPL where scientists test rovers in a Mars-like environment.

Iron: A metal that easily rusts.

Jarosite: An iron sulfate that requires water to form.

JPL: Jet Propulsion Laboratory. The place in Pasadena, California, where NASA does much of its solar system exploration work.

Lander: A spacecraft that lands on the surface of a planet.

Lava: Melted rock that flows from a volcano.

Mars Global Surveyor: The Mars orbiter launched in 1996 that relays data between the Mars rovers and Earth.

Mars Odyssey: The Mars orbiter launched in 2001 that relays data between the Mars rovers and Earth.

Mars Reconnaissance Orbiter: A Mars orbiter launched in 2006 that is capable of taking clear pictures of even small objects on the surface of Mars.

Martian year: The time it takes Mars to orbit the sun (687 Earth days).

Meteorite: A chunk of rock or meteor that has fallen to a planet's surface from space.

MI: Microscopic imager. A camera mounted on the rover's arm to take close-up photos.

Mini-TES: Miniature thermal emission spectrometer. An instrument that can determine some of the elements in a rock from a distance.

Mössbauer spectrometer: An instrument mounted on the rover's arm to identify minerals that contain iron.

NASA: National Aeronautics and Space Administration.

Navcam: Navigation camera. A black-and-white camera on the mast of Mars rovers that helps scientists see what lies ahead.

Orbiter: A spacecraft that circles a planet in its orbit.

Pancam: Panoramic camera. The high-resolution color camera on Spirit and Opportunity.

Phyllosilicates: Claylike minerals most likely to form when water is present for a long period of time.

PI: Principal investigator. The leader of the science team on a mission.

RAT: Rock abrasion tool. A tool on the rover's arm that grinds rocks to expose what is inside.

Retrorockets: Rockets that fire during final descent to push away from the landing surface, thus slowing the lander's descent.

Silica: A hard white or colorless crystallized mineral found in many rocks, soils, and sand.

Sol: One Martian day, or twenty-four hours, thirty-nine minutes, and thirty-five seconds in Earth time.

Spectrometer: An instrument that studies the radiation given off by rock or soil to determine what makes up the rock.

ndex